The Strength Within Unlocking the Secrets of Resilience

Mastering the Art of Bouncing Back and Moving Forward

Dr. Shannon A. Austin

Table of Contents

Ebook: 978-1-967124-02-2

Audiobook: 978-967124-03-9

Disclaimer Notice:

Please note the information contained within this document is for educational and entertainment purposes only. All effort has been executed to present accurate, up-to-date, reliable, and complete information. No warranties of any kind are declared or implied. Readers acknowledge that the author is not engaged in the rendering of legal, financial, medical, or professional advice. The content within this book has been derived from various sources. Please consult a licensed professional before attempting any techniques outlined in this book.

By reading this document, the reader agrees that under no circumstances is the author responsible for any losses, direct or indirect, that are incurred as a result of the use of the information contained within this document, including, but not limited to, errors, omissions, or inaccuracies.

Introduction

B efore we explore into the heart of resilience, take a moment to breathe and acknowledge the strength already present within you. Life has a way of testing our patience, our resolve, and our sense of stability —yet you have reached this point, ready and willing to learn more about weathering the storms of existence. This acknowledgment itself is a powerful testament to your inner fortitude. In these pages, we will kindle that spark and help it grow into a steady flame, guiding you through life's unpredictable terrain with greater clarity and courage.

Imagine waking up one morning to find that your alarm didn't ring, you're sporting a fresh coffee stain on your shirt, and you're already late for an important work meeting. Panic seems like the easiest option. However, what if you could transform this chaotic start into an opportunity to showcase resilience and maintain control over your day? This ability isn't a magical trait reserved for a lucky few; it's a learned skill, ready for anyone to embrace with practice.

Resilience is often misunderstood as a hidden strength that some possess while others do not. In truth, resilience doesn't mean never feeling overwhelmed or anxious; it's about recognizing these emotions without letting them define or derail you. It's about learning to navigate hardships in ways that empower rather than discourage, proving that vulnerability and strength can coexist. As we explore further, you'll discover insights that turn setbacks into stepping stones on the path to growth and fulfillment.

Think of resilience like a muscle that grows stronger with regular use. Just as exercise builds physical strength, each moment of challenge and adaptation flexes your resilience. Over time, these small, incremental efforts accumulate, forging a more flexible and responsive mindset. By reframing adversities as opportunities to learn and evolve, you'll begin to perceive each struggle not as a sign of defeat but as a stepping stone to greater confidence and inner stability.

At the core of building resilience is understanding its essence. It transcends simply bouncing back from adversity; it's the capacity to adapt, learn, and emerge stronger than before. This perspective encourages a cultural shift from viewing challenges as insurmountable roadblocks to seeing them as opportunities for personal development and transformation. Once we embrace this viewpoint, life's obstacles cease to appear intimidating; instead, they become catalysts for positive change.

Our society often clings to misconceptions about resilience, one being that only certain individuals are naturally equipped with it. Such myths stifle personal growth. By debunking these notions, we open our minds to endless possibilities for self-improvement. Recognizing resilience as a dynamic skill instead of a static trait allows us to approach difficulties with renewed optimism. It's an understanding that paves the way toward transformation, reminding us that resilience is accessible to all who choose to cultivate it.

Consider the child who learns to walk—falling countless times before finding balance and taking those first confident steps. Each tumble is not a failure but a lesson in perseverance and adaptation. Similarly, as adults, we can embrace the stumbles and setbacks we encounter. By viewing them as natural, even necessary, parts of our journey, we grant ourselves permission to grow without shame or self-judgment. This reframing nurtures resilience, reinforcing the idea that strength often emerges from our willingness to try, stumble, and try again.

Resilience is not confined to a particular stage of life. From early childhood to the later years of adulthood, opportunities abound to develop this indispensable skill. Recognizing resilience's presence across all phases of life highlights its universality. Whether we're watching a toddler adapt to a changing environment or an elder facing health challenges with poise, we witness resilience in action. Each life experience enriches our personal toolkit, preparing us to face the future with greater composure and insight.

Perhaps you wonder about the science behind resilience, where psychology meets physiology. Recent research positions resilience as a skill rooted in cognitive-behavioral principles, illuminating the brain's remarkable adaptability. Neuroscience confirms that our neural pathways can be molded and reinforced through practice. This evidence dispels the myth of innate immutability, proving instead that resilience can be intentionally developed and strengthened. Armed with this knowledge, we can approach personal growth with confidence, knowing we have the power to influence our own emotional landscapes.

Cultivating resilience extends beyond simply managing stress—it's an integral component of holistic well-being. Resilient individuals often enjoy enhanced mental health, emotional stability, and improved coping strategies. They navigate uncertainty with grace, find empathy in interactions, and approach relationships with open-hearted understanding. Ultimately, resilience doesn't merely help us endure life's trials; it enables us to thrive, forging deeper connections and a richer sense of purpose.

Real-world examples illustrate the vital role resilience plays in shaping our lives. Countless stories highlight individuals who have faced seemingly insurmountable obstacles—loss, trauma, failure—and emerged more determined, insightful, and compassionate. Such narratives transform the concept of adversity from a stumbling block into a powerful force for personal evolution, encouraging us all to view hardship as a catalyst for growth rather than a reason to surrender.

So, what drives a resilient mindset? It's rooted in embracing a growth-oriented outlook and finding hope and learning opportunities in every setback. Resilience reframes mistakes as stepping stones to success, urging us to remain open to life's lessons. By shedding the fear of error, we enter a space where curiosity and courage flourish, allowing us to transform hardship into a meaningful journey of self-discovery.

Recognizing that resilience is a continuous journey rather than a fixed destination provides both comfort and inspiration. Over time, these skills weave themselves into the tapestry of our existence, making each challenge feel more manageable and each triumph more meaningful. Through accumulated experience, resilience becomes not just a tool but a guiding principle, offering stability and assurance as we navigate life's ever-changing landscape.

As you explore deeper into this guide, you'll encounter practical exercises and empowering strategies to nurture your inner resilience. You'll learn that every setback can serve as a starting line for greater personal growth and that resilience is a potent force capable of reshaping your overall well-being. In these chapters, resilience emerges not simply as a concept but as a transformative ally—a companion that can uplift you through life's complexities.

This book is designed for anyone seeking solace and strength amidst personal or professional trials. Whether you're a stressed-out parent, a professional grappling with workplace pressure, or a seeker on the path of self-improvement, you'll find value here. With relatable scenarios, grounded insights, and compassionate guidance, you're invited to reframe your understanding of resilience—not as a lofty ideal but as a skill you can embrace and refine daily.

The path to resilience is open and inclusive, welcoming your curiosity, dedication, and eagerness to grow. As you begin this exploration, remember that the power to adapt, flourish, and move forward has always lived within you. Together, we will illuminate your journey, inspiring confidence in your ability to face life's challenges with courage, compassion, and unwavering resilience.

Chapter 1

Embracing Resilience

R esilience is a term often associated with the ability
to withstand adversity and recover from setbacks.
In today's fast-paced world, this concept is more
pertinent than ever, as individuals face an array of
personal and professional challenges. Embracing
resilience does not mean becoming hardened or unmoved
by difficulties; rather, it involves learning to navigate life's
obstacles with grace and adaptability. By approaching
hardships as opportunities to grow, resilience enables us
to transform adversity into stepping stones that strengthen
our emotional fortitude.

This chapter will reframe resilience from being an
innate trait to recognizing it as a skill that can be cultivated
and refined over time. Within these pages, readers will find
practical strategies designed to enhance their mental
resilience—accessible, research-backed techniques that
empower individuals to constructively manage adversity.
Implementing these approaches can improve overall well-
being, increase job satisfaction, and deepen interpersonal
relationships. Ultimately, embracing resilience paves the
way for meaningful personal growth, underscoring that

anyone willing to invest in these skills can thrive, even when confronted by life's most demanding circumstances.

Understanding the Basis of Resilience

Resilience is commonly understood as the ability to recover, adapt, and grow stronger in the face of hardships —whether they stem from personal setbacks, health challenges, professional difficulties, or significant societal upheavals (Fletcher & Sarkar, 2013; Maltby, Day, & Hall, 2015). At its core, resilience is not the absence of pain or struggle; rather, it encompasses acknowledging adversity, engaging with it productively, and using inner resources to move forward.

Key factors that influence how individuals adapt to adversity include:

- **Perception and Engagement:** How we interpret events and interact with our surroundings.
- **Social Resources:** The presence of supportive relationships, networks, and communities.
- **Coping Strategies:** Specific techniques employed to maintain emotional balance and stability.

These elements highlight that resilience can be developed through deliberate practice and intentional effort rather than something a person is simply born with (ADD Resource Center, 2022; Antonovsky, 1979; U.S Department of State, 2009).

The Benefits of Resilience

Developing resilience has far-reaching effects on multiple domains of life, often yielding:

- **Improved Performance and Learning:** Enhanced academic achievement and increased productivity in professional settings (Britt et al., 2016).

- **Healthier Engagement:** Lower absenteeism due to sickness and a reduced reliance on harmful coping behaviors (Johnson et al., 2011).

- **Stronger Community Ties:** Greater participation in family and community activities, fostering a sense of connection and belonging (Maltby & Hall, 2022).

- **Better Physical Health and Longevity:** Improved well-being and, in some studies, lower mortality rates (de Terte & Stephens, 2014).

Different Forms of Resilience Across the Lifespan

Resilience is not confined to any single age group or culture. It evolves as we progress through life's stages, adapting to our shifting challenges and circumstances:

- **Inherent Resilience:** Present in early childhood, guiding natural curiosity, exploration, and risk-taking.

- **Adapted Resilience:** Emerging in response to specific obstacles later in life (e.g., job loss, relationship changes), prompting rapid coping strategies.

- **Learnt Resilience:** Accumulated from past experiences, forming a robust toolkit of coping mechanisms for future adversities (Maltby, Day, Hall, & Chivers, 2019).

This continuum of resilience underscores that its capacity can expand as we mature and encounter new challenges.

Viewing resilience as a learnable skill offers a sense of agency and optimism. Unlike fixed traits one might be born with, resilience involves behaviors and attitudes anyone can nurture. Rather than perceiving adversity as a dead end, seeing it as a chance to develop coping techniques, seek community support, and strengthen mental fortitude transforms life's difficulties into opportunities for personal evolution.

Overcoming Misconceptions and Embracing a Growth Mindset

A common misconception about resilience is that it is an inherent quality accessible only to a fortunate few. In truth, resilience is more akin to a muscle that strengthens with practice and deliberate effort. By dismantling the myth of fixed resilience, we can shift from self-doubt to empowerment. Embracing a growth mindset reframes failure and hardship as opportunities for learning and improvement, rather than judgments on one's abilities (Purdue University, 2018). This perspective fosters resilience as a dynamic and attainable quality that evolves with time and experience.

When resilience is recognized as flexible and achievable, individuals gain the confidence to explore new coping strategies and adjust their perspectives. This shift promotes a cycle of continuous personal development, equipping individuals to adapt to life's transitions— whether it's starting a new career, navigating family changes, or embracing retirement—with greater ease and confidence. Resilience, at its core, is the extraordinary ability to adapt, grow stronger, and learn from adversity, developing uniquely for everyone through internal strengths and life experiences.

Common Myths About Resilience

(Davis, 2016; Wagnild, n.d.)

1. **You either have resilience or you don't.**
   Resilience is not an innate trait; it is a skill anyone can develop through practice and effort.

2. **Resilience is purely innate.**
   While some individuals appear naturally resilient, resilience is cultivated over time through life experiences and perseverance.

3. **Resilience develops in only one way.**
   Resilience is multifaceted and grows through diverse strategies, such as fostering relationships, emotional regulation, self-care, and connecting to meaning.

4. **Mindfulness is the key to resilience.**
   Though mindfulness helps some people manage stress, resilience requires personalized strategies that cater to individual needs.

5. **Resilient people handle everything on their own.**
   Supportive relationships are essential to resilience, providing emotional strength and clarity while promoting well-being.

6. **Resilience depends entirely on others.**
   While support bolsters resilience, it ultimately stems

from inner strength, as evidenced by those who thrive in isolation or adversity.

7. **Resilience is just about managing negative emotions.**
   Resilience also involves cultivating positive emotions to recover, find meaning, and build overall mental strength.

8. **Resilience means pushing through stress and illness.**
   True resilience balances recovery with effort, emphasizing the importance of rest to prevent burnout.

9. **Resilience is the same as stress management.**
   Resilience encompasses a broader mindset of purpose and persistence, going beyond traditional stress management techniques.

Resilience is not a static trait nor a skill reserved for the naturally gifted. It is a dynamic process that grows through intentional efforts and diverse strategies. By understanding and debunking the myths surrounding resilience, we can better appreciate its transformative power. Whether through personal reflection, fostering relationships, or exploring individualized coping techniques, resilience enables us to face challenges with strength and adaptability. In today's demanding world, embracing resilience as a learnable and evolving skill allows us to thrive, not just survive, in the face of adversity.

Building Resilience as a Skill

Developing resilience involves intentional practice and conscious effort. Much like learning a language or mastering a new hobby, resilience is strengthened through repeated exercises and constructive habits. Strategies that nurture resilience include maintaining perspective, accepting change, and focusing on positive outcomes. Techniques such as deep breathing, positive self-talk, and seeking guidance from mentors or counselors can also help regulate emotional responses and reinforce adaptive patterns of thinking.

Organizations stand to benefit as well. Encouraging a workplace culture that values resilience can lead to improved morale, better problem-solving, and higher productivity. Nurturing open communication, psychological safety, and supportive leadership helps team members adapt to shifting demands without fear of failure. Resilience becomes a collective asset, enhancing both individual well-being and organizational performance (Resilience and Adaptability: How You Lead Matters, n.d.).

The Science Behind Resilience

Resilience is grounded in both psychological frameworks and neuroscientific research. Cognitive behavioral principles illustrate that our responses to stress can be reshaped through introspection, learning, and practice. Meanwhile, studies in brain plasticity show that our neural pathways adapt over time, strengthening circuits that support emotional regulation, problem-solving, and stress management (Price & Duman, 2019; Yao & Hsieh, 2019).

By understanding resilience as malleable, rooted in our biology, environment, and experiences, we see that building mental toughness is accessible to everyone. Embracing resilience as a dynamic skill rather than a fixed trait encourages proactive strategies to cope with life's uncertainties, ultimately leading to greater life satisfaction, healthier relationships and improved mental well-being.

Concluding Thoughts

In this chapter, we have reframed resilience from an innate quality to a learnable skill—one that can be intentionally cultivated over time. This perspective provides hope, instilling a sense of control in individuals who may have previously felt powerless in the face of adversity. By developing resilience, people can learn to approach challenges creatively, maintain a positive mindset, and convert setbacks into growth opportunities.

The process of building resilience is rooted in practical, research-backed techniques that can be integrated into daily life. As we deepen our understanding of resilience and its underlying principles, we empower ourselves and those around us to navigate hardships with strength and flexibility. Cultivating resilience not only enriches our personal lives but also fortifies our communities, workplaces, and families, fostering environments where everyone can thrive—even amid life's inevitable storms.

Chapter 2

The Mindset Shift

S hifting your perspective on challenges can unlock a world of potential and resilience. Changing how you view obstacles is not just a theoretical concept—it's a practical tool that can transform your everyday experiences. Seeing problems as possibilities allows you to tap into hidden strengths and resources, enabling you to navigate adversity with agility and confidence. This change in mindset can significantly impact stress levels, coping mechanisms, and overall well-being. It invites you to redefine what difficulties mean to you, turning them from intimidating barriers into opportunities for growth and learning. The beauty of this shift lies in its simplicity and accessibility; anyone, irrespective of their background or circumstances, can cultivate the ability to see challenges in a new light.

In this chapter, you will explore how adopting a growth mindset empowers individuals to face various personal and professional hurdles more effectively. You will examine into the contrast between fixed and growth mindsets, examining how each influences your response to setbacks and achievements. Through practical strategies, such as self-reflection and cognitive restructuring, the chapter offers insights on nurturing adaptability and mental flexibility. You will discover techniques to foster a supportive environment that encourages creativity and experimentation, along with methods to build emotional resilience. Moreover, the importance of optimism, gratitude, and positive self-talk in maintaining a balanced outlook amidst trying times will be highlighted. As you journey through these ideas, you will gain the tools needed to harness a mindset shift, paving the way for enduring resilience and a richer, more fulfilling life.

From Fixed to Growth Mindset

Embracing a growth mindset is a transformative journey that opens the door to self-discovery, resilience, and boundless potential. The fixed mindset, often rooted in the belief that abilities are static, fosters a fear of failure and hesitation to take risks. This perspective can feel limiting, yet it provides a foundation from which growth can emerge. Challenges become opportunities to explore new paths, and mistakes transform into valuable lessons. Each misstep serves as a stepping stone toward progress, sparking curiosity and resilience. Transitioning from a fixed mindset is not about instant perfection but about celebrating small victories that collectively lead to positive transformation.

The shift to a growth mindset is an empowering process of embracing adaptability and cultivating self-belief. This mindset celebrates effort as much as outcomes, viewing challenges as exciting opportunities to expand one's capabilities. Constructive feedback, once seen as intimidating, becomes a tool for growth and self-improvement. With persistence and a willingness to learn, individuals cultivate inner confidence, replacing self-doubt with optimism and determination. Every obstacle becomes an adventure to be conquered, and every failure a stepping stone toward greater achievements. A growth mindset transforms life into a continuous journey of improvement and success.

Carol Dweck's groundbreaking work in *Mindset: The New Psychology of Success* offers an inspiring framework for understanding this transformation. The fixed mindset, characterized by avoidance of challenges and a fear of feedback, limits personal and professional growth. It thrives on the idea that intelligence and talent are fixed traits. However, Dweck emphasizes that these mindsets are fluid. With conscious effort, anyone can shift from limitations to possibilities, breaking free from self-imposed barriers. The growth mindset, in contrast, celebrates effort, persistence, and adaptability, enabling individuals to embrace challenges and turn failures into stepping stones.

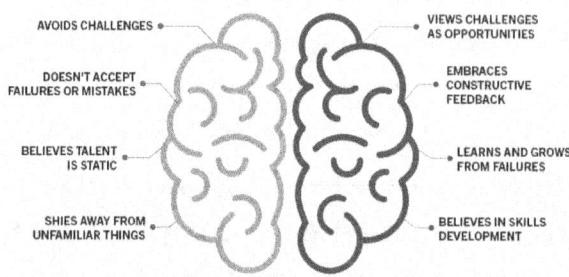

AVOIDS CHALLENGES

DOESN'T ACCEPT FAILURES OR MISTAKES

BELIEVES TALENT IS STATIC

SHIES AWAY FROM UNFAMILIAR THINGS

VIEWS CHALLENGES AS OPPORTUNITIES

EMBRACES CONSTRUCTIVE FEEDBACK

LEARNS AND GROWS FROM FAILURES

BELIEVES IN SKILLS DEVELOPMENT

Adopting a growth mindset fosters resilience, adaptability, and a passion for learning, unlocking potential in every aspect of life. By viewing intelligence and abilities as malleable, individuals and organizations create a culture of innovation and persistence. Challenges are reframed as opportunities, feedback becomes a tool for development, and success is redefined as continuous growth. Whether navigating personal challenges or striving for professional excellence, the growth mindset empowers individuals to thrive in the face of adversity and reach new heights of achievement.

To understand this transformation, it's crucial to define what constitutes both a fixed and a growth mindset. The fixed mindset operates on the belief that intelligence and abilities are static; people with this mindset view their talents as predetermined and unchangeable (Jeremiah,

2024). On the other hand, a growth mindset revolves around the idea that one's capabilities can develop through dedication and hard work. This perspective promotes a love for learning and a resilience essential for great accomplishments.

The belief in developing abilities is core to the growth mindset. It emphasizes potential beyond innate talents or resources, suggesting that effort and learning from mistakes contribute to improvement (Growth vs. Fixed Mindset: The Implications for Leadership and Innovation, 2023). For instance, rather than perceiving failure as an endpoint, a person with a growth mindset sees it as a signpost pointing toward future success. They realize that setbacks are part of the journey and provide valuable lessons about what works and what doesn't.

Conversely, the limitations of a fixed mindset become apparent when obstacles arise. Individuals with a fixed mindset often avoid challenges due to a fear of failure, which they equate with a lack of ability (Jeremiah, 2024). This avoidance limits personal and professional growth because it prevents them from taking necessary risks or experimenting with new solutions. Imagine a manager who shuns innovative projects, fearing potential criticism. This reluctance stifles creativity and prevents progress within the organization.

Self-reflection plays an integral role in shifting from a fixed to a growth mindset. By examining personal beliefs about facing challenges, individuals can identify areas where they may unconsciously limit themselves. For instance, someone might reflect on past reactions to difficult situations and recognize patterns of avoiding risk or dismissing feedback. Through introspection, it becomes possible to challenge these limiting beliefs and reframe them in ways that foster growth.

Such introspection requires honesty and openness to change. Recognizing that abilities are not set in stone encourages engagement with new challenges, turning potential roadblocks into opportunities for development. Embracing a growth mindset also involves understanding that seeking feedback and adapting strategies are proactive measures that fuel continuous improvement (Growth vs. Fixed Mindset: The Implications for Leadership and Innovation, 2023).

Moreover, cultivating a growth mindset necessitates a supportive environment. Surrounding oneself with like-minded individuals can reinforce positive behaviors and encourage resilience. In workplaces where growth mindsets are nurtured, employees feel more secure in experimenting and expressing their creativity without fear of judgment. Leaders who exemplify a growth mindset empower their teams by focusing on progress and effort rather than solely on outcomes.

This cultural shift can have profound implications, especially in high-pressure environments. Professionals in such settings, like healthcare workers or emergency responders, often face rapid changes and intense stress.

Adopting a growth mindset allows them to adapt quickly, leveraging feedback and ongoing learning to enhance performance under pressure. It transforms stress from a debilitating force into a catalyst for innovation and advancement.

Seeing Obstacles as Opportunities

In the transformative journey of reframing challenges as opportunities, a shift in mindset plays a critical role. By altering our perspectives, we can significantly reduce stress and cultivate effective coping strategies. When faced with adversity, it's common to feel overwhelmed, but viewing these situations as chances for learning rather than obstacles can be liberating. This change minimizes the psychological burden and empowers us to manage circumstances with greater calmness and clarity.

When we embrace the idea that challenges are stepping stones to growth, we open ourselves up to a plethora of possibilities. This perspective can enhance our problem-solving skills, as we become more adaptive and resourceful, finding innovative ways to tackle issues. Moreover, it encourages resilience—a crucial trait for navigating both personal and professional turbulence. Resilient individuals are not immune to difficulties; rather, they possess the ability to recover and forge ahead with renewed vigor.

Optimism is another vital element in overcoming difficulties and shifting mindsets. An optimistic outlook does not mean ignoring reality but rather maintaining confidence in one's ability to influence positive outcomes despite adversities. Optimistic individuals tend to perceive setbacks as temporary and surmountable. Research suggests that this mindset enables them to focus on solutions rather than problems, fostering perseverance even when the going gets tough (Sutton, 2019).

Gratitude and visualization are powerful strategies for altering our perception of challenges. Practicing gratitude shifts our focus from what's lacking in our lives to what we already have, creating a sense of contentment and reducing anxiety. Daily gratitude routines, such as jotting down things you're thankful for, can profoundly impact mental health by improving mood and fostering positivity. Similarly, visualization techniques empower us to imagine successful outcomes and goals, reinforcing belief in our capacity to achieve them. By regularly visualizing success, we condition our minds to stay focused and motivated, fundamentally altering how we perceive hurdles.

Incorporating journaling into our daily routine serves as both a reflective and transformative practice. Maintaining a journal allows us to track experiences, thoughts, and emotions over time. It's a space where we can process feelings, identify patterns in behavior, and document progress. Journals act as mirrors, reflecting our inner world and helping us gain insights into areas where changes in perspective might be needed. By periodically reviewing journal entries, we can acquire valuable feedback, adjust our approaches to challenges, and celebrate milestones in personal growth.

Moreover, writing about adversities can often lead to catharsis, diminishing their power over us. Articulating our struggles in words provides clarity and context, rendering complex emotions more manageable. It also creates a written record of times we've overcome past difficulties, reminding us of our strength and endurance. This practice reinforces our evolving understanding that every challenge holds within it an opportunity for growth.

Realigning beliefs and attitudes towards challenges involves actively seeking out fresh perspectives and allowing room for self-compassion and positive self-talk. Self-compassion involves treating ourselves with kindness and care, especially during tough times. Embracing self-compassion helps to soften the harsh judgments we often make about ourselves and instead fosters a supportive inner dialogue (Bradley, 2023). This internal compassion can buffer us against the negative impacts of failure by encouraging recovery rather than retreat.

Positive self-talk, akin to having a supportive coach within, is about nurturing affirming thoughts that bolster our confidence. By consciously choosing constructive language, we can counteract self-doubt and replace limiting beliefs with empowering affirmations. This approach fuels motivation and resilience, essential components for thriving amidst life's ups and downs.

Encouraging readers to reflect on their own beliefs and attitudes toward challenges is fundamental. This reflective practice can unveil ingrained thought patterns and attitudes that might be hindering growth. By examining these beliefs critically, we become more aware of the narratives we tell ourselves and can begin to rewrite them in ways that align with our aspirations and values. Such introspection paves the way for meaningful changes in how we perceive and respond to challenges.

Practical methods for fostering a growth mindset are indispensable tools in this process. Strategies like cognitive restructuring, which entails identifying and replacing negative thoughts with more constructive ones, empower us to transform our thinking patterns. Additionally, thought-stopping techniques can interrupt negativity loops, redirecting focus toward positive affirmations and empowering thoughts. These actionable steps equip us to reframe negative thoughts effectively, facilitating a mindset conducive to resilience and growth.

Strategies for Developing a Growth Mindset

A growth mindset is essential for navigating life's challenges and fostering personal development. One effective method to promote a growth mindset is reframing negative thoughts, focusing on gradual improvement. Rather than seeing setbacks as failures, consider them opportunities for growth. This approach aligns with the cognitive reframing technique, which involves altering thought patterns to uncover positive aspects within challenging situations (Vacho, 2023). For instance, after receiving critical feedback at work, shift your perspective: instead of dwelling on shortcomings, appreciate the constructive insights that can lead to professional growth.

Experimentation and learning from failures are also crucial pathways to resilience. By embracing failure as a stepping stone rather than a roadblock, individuals can cultivate a mindset open to new experiences. This method aligns with research highlighting the importance of viewing challenges as opportunities for personal development (Dealing with Negative Thoughts and Cultivating a Growth Mindset | TrainSmart Australia, 2023). Taking calculated risks, stepping out of comfort zones, and seeking diverse experiences enable the development of new skills and knowledge, ultimately strengthening resilience.

Enhanced motivation significantly benefits engagement with challenging tasks. When motivation stems from a growth-oriented perspective, it encourages persistence and effort. A growth mindset shifts focus from achieving specific outcomes to valuing the learning process itself. Celebrating small victories and recognizing effort over perfection can boost motivation, encouraging continuous progress and improvement (Vacho, 2023).

Building emotional resilience also requires consistent mindset development. Practicing self-compassion and kindness is vital in this pursuit. Treat yourself with the same understanding and support you would offer a friend. Engage in self-care activities like meditation or exercise, acknowledge accomplishments, and practice forgiveness for past mistakes. Positive self-talk can further reinforce a growth mindset by replacing critical thoughts with supportive ones (Dealing with Negative Thoughts and Cultivating a Growth Mindset | TrainSmart Australia/, 2023).

To effectively reframe obstacles, employ practical techniques such as role reversal and outcome reframing. Role reversal encourages empathy by considering others' perspectives during conflicts, fostering mutual understanding and enriched communication. Outcome reframing involves viewing setbacks as catalysts for growth, shifting focus from immediate difficulties to long-term benefits. These strategies align with the principles of learned optimism and cognitive reframing, which emphasize altering perceptions to reveal new possibilities (Vacho, 2023).

These techniques, combined with continuous practice and patience, create a foundation for enduring resilience. By consistently applying these methods, individuals can strengthen their ability to adapt and thrive amidst challenges. Developing a growth mindset is not an instant transformation but a lifelong journey marked by incremental improvements and evolving perspectives (Dealing with Negative Thoughts and Cultivating a Growth Mindset | TrainSmart Australia, 2023).

Bringing It All Together

As we've explored in this chapter, shifting from a fixed to a growth mindset can dramatically change how we confront life's challenges. This transition does not come without effort, but the rewards are profound. By embracing the belief that our abilities can be developed through dedication and hard work, we open doors to learning and resilience. A growth mindset encourages us to see setbacks not as failures, but as essential lessons on the path to success. It allows individuals to embrace challenges with curiosity and resolve, transforming obstacles into opportunities for personal and professional development.

Such a mindset shift requires self-reflection and a supportive environment. Reflecting on past experiences helps identify limiting beliefs, while surrounding oneself with others who share a growth-focused attitude can reinforce positive behaviors. Through practical techniques like cognitive restructuring and visualization, we can further cultivate resilience and adaptability. Embracing these strategies fosters a culture where persistence and effort are celebrated, nurturing emotional strength and well-being. As you continue on your journey, remember that cultivating a growth mindset is a continuous process, one that equips you to face life's ups and downs with confidence and optimism.

Chapter 3

Understanding Emotional Resilience

E motional resilience serves as our personal toolkit for navigating life's inevitable challenges. It is this capacity to recover from setbacks and adapt to difficult circumstances that allows us to thrive in a world often characterized by unpredictability and change. As we embark on this exploration of emotional resilience, consider how crucial it is in enhancing our ability not just to survive adversity but to emerge stronger and wiser. By harnessing the skills and attitudes that underpin resilience, we empower ourselves to face life's trials with a renewed sense of purpose and confidence.

This chapter examines into the multifaceted nature of emotional resilience, uncovering the key components that contribute to its development. Readers will gain insights into how self-awareness, adaptability, optimism, and support networks play pivotal roles in strengthening emotional resilience. Each section offers practical strategies to enhance these qualities, equipping individuals to better manage stress and adversity. Whether you're seeking to improve your mental fortitude or aiming to foster a more resilient mindset, the guidance provided here will serve as a valuable resource in your personal growth journey. Embrace the opportunity to build resilience, and discover how it can transform not only your life but also your approach to overcoming challenges.

Components of Emotional Resilience

Emotional resilience is a term that encapsulates our ability to bounce back from adversity and challenges. Understanding and enhancing the components of emotional resilience can help us cope better with life's ups and downs. Let's explore some critical elements that contribute to emotional resilience and discuss how we can identify and strengthen them in ourselves.

One essential component of emotional resilience is self-awareness. Self-awareness involves recognizing our emotional triggers and understanding our strengths and weaknesses. When we are self-aware, we become more attuned to how certain situations affect our emotions, which enables us to respond rather than react impulsively. This awareness allows us to manage our feelings, leading to healthier emotional responses. For example, an individual who knows that public speaking triggers anxiety can prepare by practicing deep breathing exercises beforehand. By doing so, they create a buffer zone between their emotions and their reactions, ultimately building resilience. It's also vital to recognize personal strengths—perhaps one excels in creative problem-solving or possesses strong empathy—and leverage these in challenging times to navigate obstacles effectively (Covapsychology, 2024).

Another significant element is adaptability. In an ever-changing world, being adaptable allows individuals to embrace uncertainty and respond proactively to change. Adaptable people tend to be flexible in their thinking and open to new experiences. They view setbacks not as failures but as opportunities for growth. For instance, someone who loses a job might initially feel devastated, but an adaptable mindset encourages seeing this challenge as a chance to explore new career paths or learn new skills. This approach not only eases the stress associated with unforeseen changes but also fosters innovation and creativity. Moreover, adaptability is bolstered through continuous learning and maintaining an openness to new ideas, which can further strengthen one's emotional resilience over time. (Liu et al., 2021)

An optimistic mindset is crucial for fostering psychological resilience. Optimism involves focusing on solutions rather than problems, which enhances life satisfaction and reduces stress. Optimistic individuals are more likely to find positives in negative situations, thus maintaining a sense of hope and motivation even in tough times. For example, during a demanding project at work, an optimistic person might concentrate on what could be learned from the process, rather than dwelling on the pressure involved. This positive outlook helps to build resilience by reinforcing the belief that challenges are temporary and surmountable. Practices such as gratitude journaling and reframing negative thoughts can foster optimism, encouraging a perspective that looks for the silver lining in every cloud (Covapsychology, 2024).

Strong support systems are another vital element of emotional resilience. Support systems provide shared experiences and emotional relief, reducing feelings of isolation. Having a network of family, friends, mentors, or community members offers encouragement during tough times, making it easier to manage stress and overcome challenges. A robust support system acts like a safety net; knowing there are people who care and are willing to listen can significantly alleviate emotional burdens. For example, discussing worries with a trusted friend often brings clarity and comfort, helping us feel less alone in our struggles. It's also important to engage with these networks actively, whether through regular meetups, phone calls, or participating in group activities, to maintain these bonds and reinforce mutual support. (Liu et al., 2021)

To cultivate these elements of emotional resilience, consider incorporating specific practices into your daily routine. Begin with a self-reflective practice such as journaling to enhance self-awareness. Write down daily encounters and reflect on your emotional responses to them. Identify patterns in your reactions and contemplate ways to handle similar situations positively in the future.

In terms of adaptability, try stepping out of your comfort zone regularly. Challenge yourself to learn a new skill or tackle a project that requires innovative thinking. Embrace mistakes as part of the learning process and use them to fuel further development. Additionally, nurturing an optimistic outlook can be supported by setting aside time each day to list things you are grateful for, shifting your focus away from negativity, and allowing positivity to permeate your thoughts.

Lastly, strengthen your support system by reaching out to loved ones and engaging with them frequently. Share your thoughts and feelings openly, ask for advice, and reciprocate by offering support when others reach out to you. Join clubs or communities where you share common interests, expanding your network of potential support.

Role of Emotional Intelligence

Emotional intelligence is the foundation upon which emotional resilience is built, serving as a vital mechanism for managing emotions and relationships. At its core, emotional awareness plays a crucial role in self-regulation and effective stress responses, thereby improving decision-making. Emotional awareness involves recognizing and understanding one's emotions, allowing individuals to manage their reactions more effectively. For instance, by accurately identifying feelings of anger or frustration, a person can choose appropriate ways to address these emotions, rather than acting impulsively. This ability to pause and reflect before responding can significantly impact decision-making processes, enabling more calculated and rational choices even in high-pressure situations. According to Goleman (2006), such awareness not only aids in personal growth but also enhances interactions with others by providing insights into how our emotions influence behaviors.

Empathy stands as a cornerstone of emotional intelligence, enhancing interpersonal connections and conflict resolution. By fostering collaboration and personal growth, empathy allows individuals to step into another's shoes, understanding their perspectives and emotions. This skill promotes open communication and reduces misunderstandings in both personal and professional environments. In conflict situations, empathizing with the emotions and motivations of others can lead to more constructive dialogues and solutions. For example, in a workplace setting, leaders who demonstrate empathy are better equipped to resolve disputes between team members, creating a more harmonious and productive work environment. Empathy also encourages personal development by expanding one's emotional breadth, contributing to deeper relationships and improved cooperation.

Effective self-regulation is another critical aspect of emotional intelligence that supports emotional stability and thoughtful responses instead of impulsive reactions. Self-regulation involves managing one's emotions in a healthy way, maintaining composure even amidst adversity. Those skilled in self-regulation adapt well to change and handle stress with calmness. This adaptability can be seen in professionals who maintain efficiency and clarity under pressure, making them valuable assets in any high-stress job (Craig, 2019). By practicing self-regulation, individuals can prevent negative emotions from dictating their actions, leading to more intentional and positive interactions with others. Building self-regulation skills often includes techniques such as mindfulness, cognitive reframing, and stress tolerance exercises, all of which contribute to greater emotional resilience.

Lastly, strong social skills are indispensable for navigating social complexities, enhancing leadership, and improving team effectiveness. Social skills involve the capacity to interact positively and effectively with others, drawing on an understanding of emotions to communicate and collaborate. Leaders with advanced social skills tend to foster environments where teamwork thrives, as they can motivate and inspire those around them. These leaders excel at creating bonds within teams, encouraging openness and trust, which are essential for achieving collective goals. Moreover, social skills facilitate conflict resolution by enabling clear and empathetic communication. Active listening and verbal communication are fundamental components of social skills, ensuring misunderstandings are minimized and relationships are strengthened. Developing these skills requires consistent practice and a commitment to observing and learning from social interactions.

Cultivating Emotional Resilience

Understanding emotional resilience begins with cultivating self-awareness. This crucial aspect enables individuals to recognize and understand their emotional patterns, which can lead to more effective management of emotions in challenging situations. Mindfulness practices are particularly beneficial in this endeavor, as they encourage individuals to remain present and fully engaged with the moment, helping them gain insights into their emotional responses. Regular reflection, perhaps through journaling or meditation, can further aid in identifying habitual reactions, allowing individuals to address them constructively. The practice of observing one's thoughts without judgment promotes a deeper understanding of how feelings influence behavior, which is pivotal in developing emotional resilience (Chowdhury, 2019).

Adaptability is another fundamental component in building emotional resilience. This quality involves being open to change and willing to alter approaches when faced with new challenges or shifting environments. Embracing adaptability means adopting a flexible mindset that views changes as opportunities for growth rather than obstacles. In practical terms, this could involve taking on new roles at work, learning a new skill, or adjusting personal goals in response to life changes. Such flexibility empowers individuals to navigate uncertainties effectively, reducing stress and fostering a proactive approach to problem-solving. For those in high-stress jobs, adaptability can mean the difference between thriving and merely surviving, as it allows one to maintain composure and make informed decisions even under pressure.

Nurturing optimism is a powerful tool in redirecting focus from negative experiences to positive possibilities. Gratitude practices play an invaluable role in this process. Keeping a gratitude journal, for instance, encourages individuals to document things they are thankful for, reinforcing a positive outlook even during tough times. By routinely acknowledging the good aspects of life, individuals can shift their mindset away from dwelling on problems and towards appreciating life's blessings. This shift boosts emotional resilience by enhancing life satisfaction and providing a buffer against stress. Moreover, practicing positivity through cognitive reframing—transforming negative thoughts into constructive ones—not only strengthens one's ability to see the bright side but also fosters a resilient attitude capable of weathering hard times (Covapsychology, 2024).

Building robust support networks is vital for fostering emotional resilience. Strong interpersonal relationships provide not only emotional support but also shared experiences that alleviate feelings of isolation during difficult periods. Actively connecting with family members, friends, mentors, or community organizations creates a safety net that offers both encouragement and practical assistance. These connections can be nurtured by participating in social activities, joining interest-based groups, or simply keeping in regular contact with loved ones. Such interactions promote the production of oxytocin, a hormone that calms the brain, thereby reducing anxiety and enhancing emotional stability (Chowdhury, 2019). In professional environments, fostering a collaborative team spirit can help create a supportive atmosphere where colleagues uplift each other, contributing significantly to workplace resilience.

Summary and Reflections

This chapter has investigated into the essential elements that make up emotional resilience, offering readers valuable insights into enhancing their ability to adapt and thrive amidst adversity. Through self-awareness, we've learned the significance of recognizing our emotional patterns and how this awareness can guide us to respond thoughtfully rather than react impulsively. By becoming more adaptable, we open ourselves to learning and growth opportunities, embracing life's changes with a flexible mindset. The chapter also underscores the power of optimism—finding silver linings in challenges—and highlights the importance of maintaining strong support systems to share experiences and lighten burdens.

As you reflect on these components, consider integrating them into your daily routine for a more resilient life. Whether it's through practicing self-reflection, stepping out of your comfort zone, or nurturing positive thoughts, each step strengthens your emotional foundation. Reaching out to loved ones and engaging in communities can further bolster your support network, providing a sense of security and shared strength. In embracing these practices, you're not just building resilience but also fostering a fulfilling, balanced journey, ready to face whatever comes your way with hope and determination.

Chapter 4

Stress and Adversity as Opportunities

S tress and adversity are often seen as unwelcome guests that disrupt our lives, bringing along discomfort and unease. Yet, beneath their formidable exterior lies the potential for profound personal transformation. By shifting our perspective, we can discover how these challenges are not mere obstacles but rather stepping stones that lead to growth and self-discovery. This chapter explores how reframing stress and adversity can open pathways to a deeper understanding of ourselves and enhance our ability to navigate life's unpredictability. With the right approach, stress becomes a catalyst, sparking a journey toward resilience and empowerment.

In this chapter, we examine into the biological underpinnings of stress, unveiling its role as a natural response hardwired into our bodies. We uncover how viewing stress through a new lens can turn it from an adversary into an ally, offering opportunities for learning and skill development. The chapter encompasses practical strategies for managing stress effectively, emphasizing the importance of recognizing physiological cues and employing adaptive techniques. Additionally, we examine how overcoming adversity builds confidence and sharpens problem-solving abilities, fostering mental toughness and adaptability. Empathy and personal values also emerge as vital themes, enriching our connections with others and guiding us in making purposeful decisions. Through real-life examples and evidence-based practices, this chapter aims to equip you with tools to not only manage stress but to harness it as a driver for positive change.

Reframing Stress Response

Stress is an unavoidable part of our lives, often perceived as a burden or hurdle. Yet, shifting our perspective on stress can be a pivotal step in unlocking its potential as a catalyst for personal growth. At its core, stress is a natural reaction, a response hardwired into our biology to help us face challenges and threats. By understanding this fundamental characteristic of stress, we can approach it as a manageable aspect of life rather than a crippling obstacle.

Recognizing stress as a normal, physiological reaction allows us to take proactive steps in managing it. Our bodies are designed to react to stress through mechanisms such as heightened alertness and the release of stress hormones like cortisol. While these responses can feel overwhelming, they serve a purpose; they prepare us to handle immediate challenges. By reframing our perception of these physical reactions as indicators of our body's readiness to tackle problems, we can approach stress with a more balanced mindset. This shift in viewpoint empowers individuals to embrace stress as part of the human experience, making it less daunting and more controllable.

Understanding the physiological effects of stress is crucial in reducing its negative impacts. When stressed, you might experience symptoms like tension headaches, muscle tightness, or a racing heart. These signs are your body's way of communicating that it's in a heightened state of readiness. By acknowledging these signs, you can intercept stress before it escalates into something chronic, which could lead to more serious health concerns like anxiety or depression. For instance, employing relaxation techniques such as deep breathing or progressive muscle relaxation can calm the physiological storm within, thus mitigating stress's harmful effects (7 Steps to Manage Stress and Build Resilience | Office of Research on Women's Health, n.d.).

Beyond physiological acknowledgment, viewing stress as a signal for growth creates space for personal development and adaptation. Consider stress as a cue, urging you to examine areas of personal or professional life that may require change or improvement. For example, workplace stress might highlight the need for better time management skills or assertiveness in handling tasks. By treating stress as an impetus for development, we redirect energy towards enhancing skills and capacities, facilitating evolution rather than stagnation. Training and education can play significant roles here, providing ways to adapt to stressful circumstances effectively (Bravanti, 2024).

Reframing stress from an adversary to an opportunity requires a conscious shift in mindset but can significantly enhance motivation and resilience. When one views a stressful situation not as a setback but as an opportunity to learn and grow, the outlook becomes inherently optimistic. This positive perspective doesn't just alter how we face obstacles; it transforms them into stepping stones. For instance, a project deadline once dreaded can become a chance to refine focus and productivity techniques. Such reframing fosters resilience by instilling confidence that challenges are conquerable and essential components of personal growth. In turn, this robust resilience builds the mental strength needed to face future stressors with greater assurance.

Cultivating this adaptive stress response isn't always straightforward, especially in environments or situations where stress levels are consistently high. Here, building a framework of supportive practices proves invaluable. Engaging in daily routines that prioritize self-care — like regular exercise, mindfulness practices, or simply carving out moments of joy — fortifies emotional resilience, allowing stress to become a manageable ally instead of an oppressive force. Additionally, fostering a community, whether through professional networks, friendships, or familial ties, provides reassurance and a reminder that one is not alone in navigating stress.

Guidelines for challenging negative perceptions of stress emphasize re-evaluating our initial reactions. Begin by identifying moments where stress feels debilitating and consciously choose to reinterpret those feelings as chances for growth. Practice reflecting on past situations where overcoming stress led to positive outcomes or learning experiences, reinforcing the idea of stress as an opportunity. Such practices build a resilient mindset that sees beyond immediate discomfort to long-term benefits.

To integrate stress as a driver for change, consider setting small, achievable goals that transform stress into action. For instance, if financial worries cause stress, establish a budget plan that focuses on incremental savings, turning anxiety into actionable steps a person can control. Recognizing quick wins along the journey, as minor milestones, can boost morale and encourage persistence even amid ongoing challenges.

Ultimately, adopting a positive stance towards stress involves continuous practice and commitment. Empowering ourselves with knowledge about how stress affects us biologically and psychologically lays the groundwork for reinterpreting stress in constructive ways. As we evolve in our understanding and management of stress, we light the path for others to follow, perpetuating a culture that values growth over stagnation.

Benefits of Overcoming Adversity

Overcoming adversity is not just about surviving the storms in life, but also about emerging stronger and more self-assured. Success in overcoming challenges plays a crucial role in building self-confidence. When individuals successfully navigate obstacles, their belief in their ability to handle future adversities strengthens. This sense of confidence is not only empowering but also essential for psychological resilience. It fuels a courageous mindset that sees each challenge as an opportunity to learn and grow.

Imagine someone who has faced significant hurdles, be it in personal or professional realms. As they move through these challenges and eventually overcome them, they start to recognize their own strength and capability. This recognition leads to a reinforcing cycle of self-belief – the more they succeed, the more they believe in their ability to succeed again. Self-confidence becomes a cornerstone of mental toughness, allowing individuals to tackle new problems with courage and perseverance.

Navigating difficulties does more than build confidence; it sharpens problem-solving skills, fostering adaptability through creative approaches. When facing adversity, individuals are often forced to think outside the box to find solutions, which enhances their problem-solving abilities over time. For example, a professional dealing with a challenging project may need to employ innovative methods and strategies to achieve success. This experience not only helps them solve the current problem but also prepares them for future challenges by expanding their toolkit of problem-solving techniques.

Adaptability, born from overcoming challenges, means learning to thrive in changing conditions. It involves being open to new ideas and flexible in approach. In a rapidly evolving world, this skill is invaluable. Individuals who can adapt quickly and creatively tend to excel, as they can pivot and adjust in response to unexpected twists and turns. This ability to navigate change effectively is a testament to their inner resilience and capacity for growth.

Experiencing struggles deepens empathy, fostering genuine connections and stronger support networks. When people go through tough times, they often gain a better understanding of others' challenges, enhancing their empathy. This heightened empathy enables them to connect with others on a deeper level, building stronger, more authentic relationships. These connections can provide valuable support during future hardships, creating a network of mutual aid and understanding.

Empathy derived from personal struggles allows individuals to offer support to others in a meaningful way. They can listen and respond with compassion because they have an intimate understanding of what it feels like to struggle. This shared vulnerability fosters trust and community, which are critical elements in both personal and professional settings. It helps create environments where collaboration thrives and mutual support drives personal and collective progress.

Facing challenges also reveals personal values, fostering a sense of purpose and guiding life decisions. Adversity often serves as a mirror, reflecting back our core beliefs and priorities. During difficult times, individuals are compelled to confront what truly matters to them, aligning their actions with their core values. This alignment is crucial in cultivating a sense of purpose, providing direction and motivation even amidst adversity.

Consider someone who encounters a career setback. This challenge might prompt reflection on their professional goals and personal aspirations. As they reassess their path, they might realize their true passion lies elsewhere, leading them to make significant changes aligned with their authentic selves. This clarity in values and purpose acts as a compass, guiding important life decisions and inspiring positive change.

Using Stress as a Drive for Change

Stress often enters our lives uninvited, bringing with it discomfort and uncertainty. However, when we take a step back and view stress through a new lens, it can become a surprising ally in promoting personal growth and transformation. Stress isn't merely an obstacle to overcome; it's a powerful prompt for reflection that encourages us to assess our lives deeply, leading to transformative changes that enhance our well-being.

When faced with stressors, individuals are compelled to pause and reflect on their current circumstances and paths. This reflection is not always intentional, but it acts as a necessary checkpoint where individuals can evaluate their goals, values, and priorities. It provides an opportunity to ask critical questions about whether the direction they are taking aligns with their true aspirations and desires. Reflecting on such aspects may lead to significant life adjustments, as seen in those who choose to pursue new careers or adopt healthier lifestyles after experiencing high levels of stress. These changes are not merely reactions but considered responses shaped by deeper understanding and insight, turning moments of tension into catalysts for positive change.

Stress often pushes individuals to confront truths they might otherwise avoid, serving as a motivator to pursue goals more assertively. When faced with adversity, people tap into reservoirs of determination and creativity to navigate challenges, fueling drive and motivation. The urgency accompanying stress can break down barriers that typically hold individuals back, enabling them to act decisively and exert greater effort towards achieving meaningful change. This push towards action can help individuals defy their limits, taking calculated risks that open up new opportunities and pathways previously unseen.

Challenges are unavoidable, yet they serve as essential building blocks for growth and improvement. Facing difficulties forces individuals to adapt and develop new strategies, contributing to skill enhancement and increased resilience. For instance, encountering professional burnout might inspire someone to develop time management skills or improve work-life balance, leading to enhanced productivity and job satisfaction in the long run. Such challenges encourage creative problem-solving, requiring individuals to innovate and think outside the box, ultimately leading to more robust capabilities and increased confidence in handling future adversities.

Developing adaptive techniques in response to stress is crucial, as it allows individuals to refocus energy toward positive outcomes rather than dwell on negativity. Adaptation involves recognizing stress signals and employing constructive coping mechanisms to mitigate adverse effects, such as mindfulness practices, physical activity, and maintaining strong social connections. Mindfulness, for example, helps individuals become aware of their emotions without judgment, allowing for better regulation and control over stress responses. By viewing stress as a manageable element, rather than an overwhelming force, individuals cultivate resilience, providing them with the tools needed to thrive despite hardship.

Moreover, stress can enhance resilience by teaching individuals how to rebound from setbacks with added strength and wisdom. Each encounter with stress tests one's capacity to endure, pushing boundaries and expanding comfort zones. With each challenge surmounted, individuals gain a clearer sense of their inner strength, encouraging a growth mindset that views obstacles as opportunities for learning and development rather than failures. This resilience-building process empowers individuals, reinforcing their belief in their ability to manage future challenges effectively.

Insights and Implications

This chapter sheds light on the powerful potential of stress as an agent for personal growth. By shifting our perspective, stress transforms from a daunting adversary into a valuable ally in life's journey. Recognizing stress as a natural response equips us with insight and tools to harness its energy constructively. Embracing stress allows individuals to navigate life's challenges with newfound clarity, transforming tension into stepping stones for development rather than barriers. As we shift our focus toward resilience, each stressful encounter becomes an opportunity to develop stronger, healthier coping mechanisms, ultimately leading to a more balanced and fulfilling life.

The journey of reinterpreting stress offers not just immediate relief but also long-lasting benefits. Through conscious reflection of our values and goals during stressful times, we open ourselves up to significant personal evolution. Adopting this mindset empowers us to confront difficulties with confidence and creativity, enhancing both problem-solving skills and emotional resilience. This chapter encourages readers to view stress not as a mere inconvenience but as a driving force for personal and professional advancement. Armed with this new outlook, you pave the way for continuous growth, making stress an integral part of your success story.

Chapter 5

Building a Resilient Mindset

B uilding a resilient mindset is all about nurturing
mental strength to face life's challenges with
confidence and calmness. In today's fast-paced
world, resilience is not just an asset; it's a necessity.
Whether dealing with minor setbacks or significant
adversities, building resilience offers the fortitude to
bounce back and thrive. For those navigating personal or
professional challenges, developing a strong foundation of
resilience can transform not just how obstacles are
perceived but also how effectively they are managed. As we
explore the paths to fostering this essential trait, it
becomes clear that resilience isn't a fixed skill but a
dynamic quality that grows through practice and
awareness. The journey toward a resilient mindset
involves embracing strategies that empower individuals to
overcome difficulties with optimism and grace.

This chapter delves into practical techniques that
anyone, from stressed professionals to personal
development enthusiasts, can apply in their daily lives to
enhance resilience. It covers methods such as cognitive

restructuring, which helps reshape negative thinking patterns, and gratitude journaling, a practice that shifts focus from adversity to appreciation. Readers will discover how visualization techniques can prepare the mind for success by rehearsing positive outcomes, as well as the power of affirmations in reinforcing self-belief. Each strategy is designed to contribute uniquely to a fortified mental framework, equipping individuals to tackle stress and adversity with renewed vigor. By weaving these practices into regular routines, the chapter offers tools for cultivating a more robust and adaptable mindset, ultimately enriching one's capacity to navigate life's myriad challenges.

Techniques for Positive Thinking

Psychological resilience is the ability of individuals to thrive, sustain, or regain their functionality and adaptability in the face of adversity. These adversities may include experiences of trauma, threats, or significant sources of stress (American Psychological Association [APA], 2020; Bartholomew et al., 2022; Oshri et al., 2019). Cultivating a positive mindset is an essential component of building resilience in daily life. By adopting techniques such as cognitive restructuring, gratitude journaling, visualization, and affirmations, individuals can enhance their ability to cope with stress and adversity, leading to improved mental strength and emotional well-being.

Cognitive restructuring is a powerful tool for transforming the way we perceive and respond to negative events. It involves identifying negative self-talk and challenging these thoughts before replacing them with positive affirmations. This process empowers individuals to gain control over their thoughts and emotions, fostering a more resilient mindset. For instance, when faced with the thought, "I always fail," cognitive restructuring encourages reframing this idea into something constructive like, "I have succeeded before and can learn from my mistakes." This shift not only reduces stress but also enhances one's confidence in overcoming future challenges (Calm Blog Team, 2023).

Gratitude journaling is another effective technique that helps redirect focus from adversity to appreciation. By regularly writing down things one is grateful for, whether as simple as a sunny day or as profound as a supportive friend, individuals train their minds to notice the good in life, rather than dwelling on the negatives. This practice is a counterbalance to the brain's natural inclination towards negativity, enhancing emotional well-being and resilience. Research has shown that consistent gratitude practice can significantly improve happiness and overall mental health (Calm Blog Team, 2023). As a guideline, try setting aside a few minutes each day to jot down at least three things you are thankful for.

Visualization techniques serve as mental rehearsals that prepare the mind for overcoming obstacles. By vividly imagining positive outcomes, individuals can reduce anxiety and foster a proactive mindset. Visualization is frequently employed by athletes to enhance performance, but it is equally valuable for everyday challenges. Engaging all the senses during visualization, such as picturing oneself successfully achieving a goal while feeling the emotions of triumph, creates a mental roadmap for success. This not only boosts motivation but also builds self-efficacy, encouraging individuals to face challenges with confidence (NYC Integrative Psych, n.d.). To maximize the benefits, visualize daily in a quiet environment where concentration can be maintained.

Affirmations and positive self-talk play a crucial role in creating an emotional foundation that supports resilience. By consistently reinforcing positive beliefs about oneself, individuals can rewire their brains to embrace challenges confidently. The practice of affirming one's strengths and capabilities transforms the internal dialogue from doubt to encouragement. Over time, this adaptation results in greater mental resilience, allowing for the confrontation of life's adversities with optimism and tenacity (Explore Psychology, 2017). It's helpful to identify personal strengths and use these as anchors for your affirmations, repeating them throughout the day.

These positive thinking strategies do not operate in isolation; they complement each other to foster a robust mental framework capable of withstanding pressures and setbacks. The interconnectedness of cognitive restructuring, gratitude, visualization, and affirmations illustrates how cultivating a positive thinking habit can significantly enhance resilience in everyday life. These practices collectively contribute to a fortified mindset where challenges are seen not as insurmountable barriers but as opportunities for growth and learning. In essence, developing a positive thinking habit lays a solid foundation for lifelong resilience, equipping individuals to navigate personal and professional stresses with unwavering strength (NYC Integrative Psych, n.d.).

For individuals experiencing stress or adversity, professionals in high-stress environments, or those interested in personal development, integrating these strategies into daily routines can markedly improve mental resilience. Whether through morning affirmations, evening gratitude reflections, or midday visualizations, the key lies in consistency and intentional practice. Over time, these techniques become second nature, fundamentally altering how one perceives and responds to life's challenges.

Building Mental Strength

Developing a resilient mindset is crucial for navigating life's challenges effectively. One foundational element in this journey is emotional regulation, an invaluable skill that helps individuals recognize and manage their emotional responses. By honing this ability, people can enhance focus and improve decision-making under stress, ultimately leading to better outcomes in various aspects of life. Techniques such as mindfulness meditation, deep breathing exercises, and journaling are practical strategies for cultivating emotional regulation. These techniques allow individuals to pause and reflect before reacting, providing a momentary buffer against impulsive actions prompted by heightened emotions (Mental Strength: 8 Ways to Build Resilience, 2023).

In addition to managing emotions, setting realistic goals plays a vital role in building mental fortitude. When faced with challenges, having clear and achievable goals fosters a sense of direction and purpose. Breaking down larger objectives into smaller, manageable steps creates a roadmap for progress, reinforcing belief in one's capabilities and boosting confidence. This approach not only aligns one's endeavors with their values but also ensures that each milestone reached further solidifies the conviction that they can overcome obstacles and achieve desired outcomes (gliapko@havenhealthmgmt.org, 2024). For instance, if someone aims to run a marathon, starting with short-distance runs and gradually increasing the distance allows them to see tangible progress, making the ultimate goal seem more attainable.

Perseverance training is another pivotal strategy for developing a resilient mindset. Embracing challenges with determination gradually builds a resilient spirit and foundational confidence. Training oneself to persist through difficulties involves cultivating grit—the ability to maintain effort and interest over long periods despite setbacks. Approaching challenges as opportunities for growth rather than insurmountable barriers transforms failures into valuable learning experiences (Mental Strength: 8 Ways to Build Resilience, 2023). Consider a professional facing a challenging project; instead of viewing initial failures as roadblocks, they may see them as stepping stones toward mastering new skills, thus enhancing their competence and confidence.

Self-compassion practices also contribute significantly to mental resilience. Being kind to oneself during moments of failure or self-doubt is essential for maintaining mental strength. Self-compassion involves recognizing that setbacks are a natural part of life and responding to them with understanding and kindness rather than harsh criticism. Practicing self-compassion fosters a nurturing mindset that aids swift recovery from adversity and bolsters emotional health (Gliapko, 2024). For example, when an individual makes a mistake at work, treating themselves with the same empathy they would offer a friend enables them to learn from the experience without internalizing it as a reflection of their worth.

The integration of these strategies—emotional regulation, setting realistic goals, perseverance training, and self-compassion practices—creates a robust framework for developing resilience. Emotional regulation provides the clarity needed to navigate stressful situations calmly, while setting realistic goals offers a structured path to achieving personal and professional aspirations. Perseverance training encourages facing challenges head-on, fostering a growth-oriented mindset. Simultaneously, self-compassion ensures that setbacks are met with empathy, preventing negative self-talk from hindering progress.

Each of these elements contributes uniquely to building mental fortitude. Emotional regulation enhances one's ability to remain composed under pressure, enabling more effective problem-solving and decision-making. It acts as a stabilizing force amid chaos, allowing individuals to respond with intention rather than reaction. Through consistent practice, emotional regulation becomes a habitual response, fostering resilience even in the face of unexpected challenges.

Setting realistic goals is not merely about ambition; it's about strategic foresight and practicality. Goals that are too lofty may lead to frustration and burnout, whereas overly simplistic ones might fail to inspire growth. By establishing clear, attainable objectives that align with personal values, individuals create a motivational cycle that sustains their efforts. Achieving these goals provides a sense of accomplishment and fuels continued perseverance, encouraging individuals to tackle increasingly complex challenges.

Perseverance training reinforces the notion that resilience is built over time through persistent effort. It underscores the value of grit—the tenacity to push forward despite setbacks. By embracing failures as opportunities for growth, individuals develop a positive relationship with adversity. They learn to adapt, recalibrate their approaches, and persist until they succeed. This adaptability not only strengthens their resolve but also broadens their problem-solving abilities.

Self-compassion acts as a safeguard against the detrimental effects of negative self-criticism. It nurtures a supportive inner dialogue that acknowledges human fallibility and emphasizes growth over perfection. During difficult times, self-compassion provides the reassurance needed to weather storms without succumbing to feelings of inadequacy. This practice fosters an environment where learning from mistakes becomes a catalyst for improvement rather than a source of shame.

Combining these strategies into daily routines requires intentionality and patience. Just as physical fitness demands regular exercise, mental resilience develops through consistent practice. Incorporating moments of mindfulness, reflection, and goal-setting into one's day can transform how challenges are perceived and addressed. Over time, these practices cultivate a resilient mindset that not only withstands adversity but thrives in its presence.

Developing Emotional Resilience

In today's fast-paced world, emotional resilience is not just a desirable trait but a necessary one. It enables individuals to manage stress and adversity with poise and strength. By integrating practical strategies such as mindfulness meditation, fostering supportive relationships, employing effective stress management techniques, and adapting to change, we can equip ourselves to handle life's inevitable challenges with grace.

Mindfulness meditation is a powerful tool for cultivating emotional resilience. This practice involves paying attention to the present moment in a non-judgmental way, which helps individuals develop greater awareness of their feelings and thoughts. When you engage in mindfulness meditation, you enhance your ability to accept emotions as they arise rather than suppressing them, which can lead to increased calmness and reduced stress. In fact, studies have shown that regular mindfulness practices can decrease symptoms of anxiety and depression, making it easier to navigate stressful situations with clarity and focus (National Institutes of Health, 2022).

Another essential component of building emotional resilience is establishing a robust support network. Human beings are inherently social, and having meaningful connections with others can provide significant emotional benefits, especially during challenging times. A strong support network offers diverse perspectives and insights that can help you see problems from different angles, leading to more adaptable solutions. Engaging in community activities or joining support groups can reinforce these connections, enabling you to draw strength from shared experiences and mutual encouragement (Mental Health Center of San Diego, 2024).

Stress management techniques also play a crucial role in developing resilience. Techniques such as deep breathing, progressive muscle relaxation, and guided imagery can effectively regulate your physiological responses to stress, enhancing your coping capacity. For instance, taking a few moments to practice deep breathing when feeling overwhelmed can lower heart rate and blood pressure, allowing you to approach problems with a clearer mind. These strategies empower individuals to manage stress proactively, rather than letting it dictate their reactions (National Institutes of Health, 2022).

Adaptability is another cornerstone of emotional resilience. Life is unpredictable, and learning to adapt to change and uncertainty can significantly bolster your resilience. Being flexible and resourceful enables you to pivot and find new pathways when faced with obstacles. Developing an adaptive mindset involves embracing change as an opportunity for growth rather than a threat. By viewing challenges through this lens, you cultivate a resilient spirit that is better prepared to handle whatever comes your way.

Incorporating these strategies into daily life requires commitment, but the rewards are well worth the effort. Start by dedicating a small amount of time each day to practicing mindfulness meditation. Find a comfortable space to sit quietly, close your eyes, and focus on your breath. Notice any thoughts or feelings that arise without judgment, simply acknowledging them and returning your focus to your breath. Over time, you'll likely find that you're able to bring this mindful presence into other areas of your life, helping you remain centered in stressful situations.

Building a support network might involve reaching out to friends, family, or colleagues to strengthen existing relationships or explore new ones. Participating in group activities or volunteering can introduce you to like-minded individuals who share your interests and values. Remember that these connections are reciprocal—offering support to others often strengthens the bonds you have.

To integrate stress management techniques, consider scheduling short sessions throughout your day to practice deep breathing or relaxation exercises. Even a few minutes can make a noticeable difference in your stress levels, helping you maintain focus and resilience under pressure. Experiment with different techniques to discover what works best for you, and don't hesitate to consult resources or professionals if you need guidance.

Finally, nurture your adaptability by embracing change rather than resisting it. Challenge yourself to view setbacks as opportunities to learn and grow. Reflect on past experiences where you successfully navigated change and draw on those insights in future situations. The more you practice adaptability, the more naturally it will come when faced with adversity.

Summary and Reflections

In this chapter, we explored practical strategies for developing resilience through positive thinking and mental strength. Techniques like cognitive restructuring, gratitude journaling, visualization, and affirmations empower individuals to cultivate a more optimistic mindset. These tools not only help in shifting perspectives but also enhance emotional well-being and confidence when facing challenges. By regularly practicing these techniques, readers can transform negative thoughts into constructive ones, fostering resilience as they navigate life's ups and downs. Additionally, mindfulness meditation, emotional regulation, goal-setting, perseverance training, and self-compassion are highlighted as key components in building mental fortitude. Together, these practices create a strong framework for managing stress and adversity with grace and strength.

The chapter emphasized the integration of these strategies into daily routines, encouraging consistency and intentional practice to achieve lasting results. By adopting a routine that includes morning affirmations, evening gratitude reflections, or midday visualizations, individuals can create new habits that support resilience. Emotional regulation and setting realistic goals were underscored as ways to maintain focus and motivation, while perseverance training fosters grit and adaptability. Practicing self-compassion ensures setbacks are met with understanding rather than criticism, promoting recovery and growth. Ultimately, these practical approaches equip readers to handle personal and professional pressures with unwavering strength and optimism, leading to a more resilient and fulfilling life.

Chapter 6

Developing Coping Mechanisms

C rafting effective coping mechanisms is pivotal for building resilience, and it opens pathways to managing stress with greater ease. The ability to navigate life's challenges often hinges on understanding the diverse strategies available and choosing those that align best with personal needs. Coping mechanisms are like a personalized toolkit, each tool providing unique support for different situations. Whether dealing with professional pressures or personal adversities, having an array of strategies ready can transform potential obstacles into manageable tasks. Embracing a proactive approach allows individuals to face stress head-on, fostering not only immediate relief but also long-term growth and adaptation. By actively engaging with these techniques, people can cultivate a mindset geared towards positivity and endurance, essential traits for thriving amidst life's unpredictability.

In this chapter, we delve into the various types of coping strategies, examining their roles in boosting resilience. Readers will explore problem-focused tactics that tackle stressors directly, offering practical solutions for changeable situations. Alternatively, when faced with unavoidable circumstances, emotion-focused strategies provide tools for managing emotional responses effectively. The nuances of avoidance coping, both its pitfalls and occasional benefits, will be unpacked to help recognize when disengagement might offer temporary solace without fostering negative patterns. Social support as a key strategy underscores the significance of relationships in alleviating stress and reinforcing shared resilience. By incorporating these varied approaches into everyday life, individuals can enhance their capacity to withstand stress while enriching their personal growth journey. This exploration aims to equip readers with the knowledge to employ adaptive coping strategies tailored to their unique contexts, ultimately leading to a more resilient and balanced life.

Different Types of Coping Strategies

Developing effective coping strategies is essential for enhancing resilience and managing stress. By understanding the various approaches to coping, individuals can build a robust toolkit that supports them in navigating life's challenges with greater ease and confidence.

Problem-focused coping is one key strategy that involves addressing the root cause of stress directly through problem-solving techniques. This approach aims to prevent stress from escalating by actively engaging with the stressor. For instance, if someone faces work-related stress due to an overwhelming workload, they can use time management skills or delegate tasks to mitigate the pressure. Such proactive measures help reduce the stressor's impact and empower individuals to regain control over their situations (Algorani & Gupta, 2023). Problem-focused coping is most effective when the stressor is within our capacity to change, allowing us to implement practical solutions that resolve or lessen the issue at hand.

Emotion-focused coping shifts the focus from the stressor itself to the emotions it triggers. Instead of attempting to alter the situation, this approach helps individuals manage their emotional reactions. Techniques such as cognitive reframing, meditation, and breathing exercises are valuable tools in fostering emotional awareness and adaptability. By reinterpreting a stressful event more positively, people can alter their emotional responses, reducing anxiety and enhancing resilience. An example is using humor or positive self-talk to diffuse tension during a presentation. Emotion-focused coping is particularly beneficial when dealing with unavoidable stressors, enabling individuals to maintain their well-being even when circumstances cannot be changed (Bartel, Sherry, & Stewart, 2020).

Avoidance coping identifies unhealthy patterns where disengagement might initially seem appealing but can become detrimental over time. This style includes behaviors such as denial or procrastination, which can exacerbate stress rather than alleviate it. However, there are instances when temporary disengagement is beneficial for mental well-being. For example, taking a short break from a heated argument provides space to calm down and return with a clearer perspective. Understanding when avoidance serves as a healthy pause rather than a destructive habit is crucial. Recognizing and modifying these patterns helps prevent long-term adverse effects and encourages healthier coping mechanisms overall (Ackerman, 2017).

Social support strategies highlight the importance of leveraging relationships for emotional support. These strategies involve reaching out to friends, family, or colleagues to share experiences and seek encouragement and advice. Social networks serve as a buffer against stress, providing a sense of belonging and reassurance during difficult times. Whether it's confiding in a friend or participating in group activities, social connections offer invaluable emotional sustenance. For professionals in high-stress jobs, turning to peers who understand similar pressures can reinforce solidarity and shared resilience. Building and maintaining supportive relationships not only alleviate stress but also foster a collective strength that enhances community resilience (Nevill & Havercamp, 2019).

Incorporating these diverse coping strategies into daily life requires intentional practice and self-awareness. While problem-focused and emotion-focused coping provide actionable steps for individuals to address stress proactively, understanding the nuances of avoidance coping ensures that disengagement is constructive rather than harmful. Simultaneously, cultivating social support networks bolsters individual resilience while enriching the wider community. By integrating these approaches, individuals create a personalized toolkit tailored to their unique needs and circumstances.

Learning to adaptively deploy different coping strategies based on the context is vital for developing resilience. Each method offers distinct benefits and is suited to specific situations, allowing for flexible responses to life's myriad stressors. Embracing this versatility empowers individuals to thrive despite adversity, strengthening their emotional intelligence and mental fortitude.

Implementation of Coping Techniques

Integrating effective coping techniques into daily life forms a strong foundation for resilience. As stressors arise, having a structured plan in place allows you to manage challenges with greater ease. One effective way to foster this resilience is by creating a coping plan. This involves identifying potential stressors and outlining strategies specific to handling these situations. By anticipating potential difficulties and preparing responses, you transform stress into an expected event rather than a surprise burden. For example, if work deadlines or family obligations are common stressors, your plan might include regular time management reviews or designated breaks to mitigate their impact. Creating such a plan not only helps manage existing stress but also equips you to navigate future unpredicted challenges effectively (7 Steps to Manage Stress and Build Resilience | Office of Research on Women's Health).

Daily practice of coping techniques is essential for turning these strategies into habits that seamlessly integrate into your lifestyle. Consistency is crucial; the more routinely you engage in these techniques, the more naturally they become part of your routine. Practices such as mindfulness meditation, exercise, or even brief moments of deep breathing can significantly enhance your resilience over time. This approach aligns with findings that consistently practiced techniques help reduce tension and promote relaxation, contributing to an overall sense of well-being. Embedding these practices into daily life, much like brushing your teeth or preparing meals, ensures that resilience-building becomes second nature. Such integration doesn't require drastic life changes—a few minutes dedicated each day can make a considerable difference (Newman, 2016).

Monitoring and reflection are key components in understanding the effectiveness of your coping mechanisms. Regular assessment enables you to determine which strategies are working and where adjustments might be needed. Keeping a journal or using tracking apps can facilitate this process by providing insight into patterns and progress over time. This practice not only promotes self-awareness but also encourages adaptability by pinpointing areas that need reinforcement or change. Reflecting on successes and setbacks can illuminate paths to improvement and reinforce the importance of self-care and personal growth. By understanding what works best for you, adapting your coping strategies becomes an informed, intentional process.

Seeking professional guidance offers the opportunity to access advanced tools and tailored strategies that enhance your ability to cope effectively. Experts can provide personalized approaches based on your unique experiences and needs. This could involve therapy sessions focused on cognitive-behavioral techniques, workshops on stress management, or support groups that offer shared experiences and insights. Engaging with professionals not only broadens the spectrum of available resources but also supports continuous resilience growth through expert intervention. Recognizing when to seek such guidance reflects a proactive commitment to mental health and well-being, boosting your confidence in managing life's stressors.

Strategies for Building Emotional Resilience

To build lasting emotional resilience, it's vital to understand and implement strategies that strengthen our capacity to withstand life's challenges. Emotional awareness lies at the heart of resilience. It's not merely about identifying feelings but developing a deep understanding of how these emotions affect our thoughts and actions. Such awareness is crucial because it allows us to navigate through stress by acknowledging and processing our emotions rather than being overwhelmed by them. For instance, recognizing when you're feeling anxious can lead you to take steps such as journaling or speaking with someone you trust, which helps alleviate the burden. This kind of mental adaptation enhances not only personal strength but also adaptability in various circumstances. (Chowdhury, 2019)

Another cornerstone of emotional resilience is mindfulness practices. These techniques, including meditation and deep breathing, focus on cultivating an awareness of the present moment. The benefit here is twofold: first, mindfulness helps reduce stress by diverting focus from overwhelming thoughts, and second, it builds emotional control. When practicing mindfulness, you train your mind to observe thoughts without judgment, allowing for more measured responses rather than impulsive reactions in stressful situations. A simple practice like setting aside five minutes each day for mindful breathing can make a significant difference in emotional regulation. As Buddha said, "The secret of health for both mind and body is...to live in the present moment wisely and earnestly." By doing so, we can better manage life's unpredictability. (Group, 2024)

Cultivating a growth mindset also plays a pivotal role in resilience. This approach involves viewing challenges as opportunities rather than setbacks, promoting perseverance and determination. A growth mindset empowers individuals to embrace failure as a learning experience, fostering an environment where emotional fortitude can thrive. For example, if a project at work doesn't succeed as planned, instead of seeing it as a defeat, one might look at it as a chance to gain new insights and improve skills. This positive approach encourages continuous personal development and the resilience to bounce back from adversity.

In addition to mindset changes, surrounding ourselves with supportive relationships greatly contributes to emotional resilience. Positive relationships provide a much-needed buffer against life's stresses by offering encouragement, support, and shared experiences. Engaging with friends, family, or community groups can bolster your sense of belonging and offer fresh perspectives during challenging times. Having a trusted network acts as a safety net, providing reassurance and guidance when faced with difficulties. Regularly nurturing these connections through open communication and shared moments strengthens both the bonds and the individual's resilience.

Gratitude practices further enhance resilience by shifting focus from what's lacking to appreciating what exists. Keeping a gratitude journal can serve as a daily reminder of positives in life, encouraging a more optimistic outlook. This habitual practice can increase emotional well-being and provide stability during turbulent times. Similarly, expressing gratitude within interpersonal relationships can encourage stronger emotional connections, enhancing mutual support and resilience. Gratitude becomes not just an internal exercise but a bridge-building tool with others, promoting communal resilience and wellbeing.

Moreover, integrating self-care routines within our daily lives supports the foundation of emotional resilience. Self-care isn't just about physical upkeep; it encompasses mental and emotional nurturing as well. Activities such as regular exercise, balanced nutrition, and adequate rest help maintain overall health, while engaging in hobbies or relaxation techniques can rejuvenate the mind. Simply put, taking time for oneself replenishes the energy needed to face life's demands with renewed vigor.

Lastly, facing fears and embracing vulnerability are essential for building resilience. Often, it's easy to shy away from difficult situations or uncomfortable emotions. However, confronting these head-on allows for personal growth and increased confidence in managing future adversities. Whether attempting a daunting task at work or addressing a conflict in a relationship, stepping out of comfort zones leads to a broader perspective and a reinforced sense of capability. Understanding that vulnerability is part of the human experience and accepting it can transform challenges into stepping stones for resilience.

Reflection

In this chapter, we've delved into crafting strategies that bolster resilience, equipping you with a variety of coping techniques to face life's stressors. We've explored problem-focused coping, which empowers you to tackle the root causes of stress through practical solutions, and emotion-focused coping, which aids in managing feelings stirred by stressors, enhancing emotional intelligence and adaptability. Understanding avoidance coping has illustrated when disengagement serves positively rather than hindering progress. Additionally, social support strategies underscore the invaluable role relationships play in cushioning stress's impact. This comprehensive approach encourages building a personalized toolkit suited to your circumstances, fostering both individual resilience and a sense of community strength.

As we wrap up this discussion, it's clear that integrating these diverse coping methods into everyday life is crucial for nurturing resilience. Developing a structured coping plan helps anticipate and navigate challenges smoothly, turning potential stress into manageable tasks rather than unforeseen obstacles. The consistent practice of mindfully chosen techniques transforms them into habitual responses, promoting a resilient mindset. By regularly assessing and adapting these strategies, you enhance your ability to cope effectively, supported by robust social networks and guided by professional insights when needed. Embracing this adaptable approach to coping not only fortifies mental fortitude but also enriches your personal development journey, equipping you to thrive amid adversities with optimism and strength.

Chapter 7

The Power of Positive Habits

D eveloping positive habits is a powerful way to fortify one's resilience against life's inevitable challenges. These daily practices, though seemingly small in scale, collectively build a stronger foundation for mental and emotional well-being. As individuals strive to adapt and flourish, the power of consistent routine becomes apparent through its subtle yet profound influence on how we handle stressors. Habits shape our responses to adversity, turning the unpredictable chaos of life into a more manageable series of events. By recognizing the impact of these habitual patterns, we can tap into an internal reservoir of strength that transforms even the most daunting situations into opportunities for growth.

This chapter explores the vital role habits play in cultivating resilience. It delves into how structured routines and intentional physical activities can significantly bolster mental clarity and emotional stability. Readers will uncover valuable insights into the importance of reflection and mindfulness as avenues for enhanced self-awareness and coping mechanisms. The discussion extends to the nurturing aspects of healthy eating choices, illustrating how nutrition directly influences cognitive functions and mood. Throughout, practical strategies are offered for implementing positive habits tailored to individual needs, ensuring these transformative practices are sustainable and meaningful. By the end, readers will be equipped with knowledge and actionable tactics to embrace empowering routines that enhance their capacity to thrive amid life's unpredictability.

Creating Empowering Routines

In today's fast-paced world, establishing positive routines is an effective way to build resilience and bring predictability to daily life. The power of a structured routine lies in its ability to provide a comforting rhythm that reduces anxiety and enhances decision-making. A morning routine, for example, serves as a cornerstone in setting this positive tone. By starting the day with consistency—whether it's through meditation, exercise, or a set breakfast—the mind is primed to handle challenges calmly and rationally. When decisions are less burdensome, individuals experience elevated moods and make healthier choices throughout the day (Robins, n.d.).

Carving out time for reflection is another vital component of resilience. Engaging in daily journaling or mindfulness practices enables individuals to process emotions effectively. Over time, these habits lead to greater self-awareness and improved coping strategies. Reflection helps identify patterns of thought and behavior that may be hindering personal growth. By understanding these patterns, one can better navigate adversities and enhance emotional intelligence, fostering a resilient mindset.

Physical activity also plays a crucial role in fortifying resilience. Incorporating exercise into daily routines releases endorphins, the body's natural mood lifters, which significantly boost mental health. Activities like walking, jogging, or yoga not only increase energy levels but also instill discipline and focus. As regular exercise becomes habitual, it transforms into a source of strength, both physically and mentally, empowering individuals to face life's obstacles with confidence. According to research, while forming such habits may take longer than simpler ones—often ranging from 66 to over 200 days—the benefits are substantial when tailored to individual needs and consistently practiced (Arlinghaus & Johnston, 2018).

Equally important is maintaining healthy eating habits, which directly affect cognitive function and mood stability. Consuming nutritious foods at regular intervals not only nourishes the body but also supports mental clarity and emotional equilibrium. This stable foundation empowers people to make better food choices naturally, contributing to enhanced resilience. Much like other routines, the key to success lies in persistence and recognizing that occasional deviations won't derail progress. Perfect adherence isn't necessary; rather, building lasting routines encourages long-term well-being (Arlinghaus & Johnston, 2018).

Creating empowering routines involves intentional planning and gradual implementation. Setting realistic goals and celebrating small victories help cement new habits. Tailoring routines to fit individual lifestyles ensures greater adherence and enjoyment, turning each day's structure into a source of empowerment.

By dedicating consistent time for reflection, individuals nurture their inner world, creating space for healing and growth. Whether through meditation, therapy, or personal introspection, this practice allows for the processing of complex emotions, leading to insightful revelations and the development of adaptive coping mechanisms. In times of stress, having a reliable outlet for thoughts and feelings enhances resilience by preventing overwhelming emotions from taking control.

Physical activity, as part of these routines, acts as a powerful antidepressant and energy booster. It doesn't require strenuous workouts to reap benefits; even moderate activities like brisk walking or dancing can invigorate the mind and stabilize emotions. Incorporating movement into daily life promotes discipline, helping individuals stick to their commitments and face challenges head-on. The sense of accomplishment and well-being following physical exertion reinforces the cycle of positivity and resilience.

Nourishing the body with wholesome foods plays a pivotal role in maintaining a resilient mind and spirit. A balanced diet rich in vitamins, minerals, and antioxidants supports brain health, enhances memory, and stabilizes emotions. The act of choosing nutrient-dense meals also cultivates discipline and mindfulness, strengthening one's resolve to pursue a resilient lifestyle. Embracing dietary habits that promote vitality ensures sustained energy levels, enabling individuals to tackle daily tasks with vigor and clarity.

Routines offer a sanctuary of predictability amid life's uncertainties. They provide a structure that anchors individuals during turbulent times, minimizing stress and overwhelm. By embedding positive habits into daily life, people create a foundation of stability that supports thriving amidst adversity. A carefully crafted routine doesn't just fill time; it enriches life with purpose and intention.

Incorporating routine-building techniques into daily life promotes long-term health and resilience. Simple strategies like preparing meals in advance, scheduling workouts with friends, or setting aside time for reflection can drastically reduce the number of decisions faced each day. Fewer decisions mean less mental fatigue and more energy to dedicate to meaningful pursuits. This deliberate approach to routine creation fosters an environment where resilience flourishes and life's challenges become opportunities for growth.

Breaking Negative Habitual Patterns

In the journey toward building resilience, one of the most crucial steps is identifying and breaking free from negative habits that hinder our ability to adapt to challenges. Understanding how these habits function can empower us to create a more adaptive and resilient mindset, allowing for greater self-awareness and emotional strength.

The first step in this process involves recognizing the triggers that activate negative habits. Triggers can be specific situations, emotions, or even people that prompt the onset of unwanted behaviors. By identifying these triggers, individuals can anticipate their responses and develop strategies to manage them effectively. For example, someone might notice that stressful work environments trigger overeating as a coping mechanism. With this recognition, they can plan healthier responses, such as taking a short walk or practicing deep breathing techniques when stress arises (Mayo Clinic Staff, 2020).

To illustrate, let's consider Lisa, who noticed that her habit of procrastination intensified whenever she felt overwhelmed by work deadlines. Rather than succumbing to this cycle, Lisa began journaling her feelings each time she faced a deadline, helping her understand the root cause of her procrastination. This self-awareness allowed her to develop practical steps to counteract the habit, such as breaking tasks into smaller, manageable parts.

Once triggers are acknowledged, the next step is learning replacement strategies, which involve substituting negative actions with constructive activities. This aspect is pivotal in creating a healthier feedback loop, where positive reinforcements replace negative patterns. Consider adopting hobbies or engaging in creative pursuits as a means to steer away from negative habits. For instance, turning to art, reading, or gardening instead of falling back on old detrimental behaviors establishes new pathways for handling stress or adversity (Newman, 2016).

Take John, a professional under constant work pressure, who used smoking as a stress reliever. Acknowledging this, he took up jogging each morning. Gradually, the endorphin release from running provided a natural high, replacing the temporary relief smoking offered. Over time, jogging became not just a stress management tool but a core part of his day, helping him stay grounded and focused.

A critical component of modifying habits lies in establishing accountability systems. Having support from friends, family, or groups can significantly impact one's commitment to breaking negative patterns. These systems provide encouragement, motivation, and a sense of responsibility towards shared goals. For example, joining a group focused on health improvement can encourage members to share progress, celebrate successes, and offer advice during setbacks, reinforcing a collective effort toward personal development (Mayo Clinic Staff, 2020).

For Rachel, overcoming her late-night snacking habit seemed daunting until she enlisted the help of a friend who shared similar goals. Together, they set up nightly check-ins, sharing what they ate and encouraging each other to make healthier choices. This mutual support built a strong accountability structure, making the transition smoother and more enjoyable.

Understanding gradual change is crucial in avoiding overwhelm and encouraging sustainable behavior shifts. Many people fall into the trap of attempting drastic changes, only to find the burden too heavy to maintain long-term. Real resilience development comes through steady, incremental progress where each small victory builds toward larger goals. It's about appreciating the journey and recognizing each step as an achievement (Newman, 2016).

Consider the case of Tom, a professional struggling with work-life balance. Attempting to overhaul his routine overnight left him feeling exhausted and defeated. Instead, he decided to introduce minor adjustments weekly, like dedicating an hour in the evening to non-work activities. This approach allowed Tom to gradually adapt without undermining his daily responsibilities, finally achieving a stable balance that supported his overall well-being.

Moreover, people seeking to develop resilience must understand that setbacks will occur. Viewing these as learning opportunities rather than failures fosters a mindset geared toward growth and persistence. Each setback provides valuable insights into what works and what doesn't, offering guidance for future endeavors.

Establishing Resilient Mindsets

Harnessing the power of positive habits begins with cultivating a mindset that enhances resilience through adaptability and positivity. Developing a growth mindset is foundational for building resilience. It enables individuals to view challenges as opportunities for learning rather than insurmountable obstacles. A growth mindset encourages one to embrace failures as stepping stones towards success and improvement.

Consider how setbacks can be reframed as valuable lessons. For instance, when faced with a project that didn't go as planned at work, analyzing what went wrong and understanding the growth areas can transform the experience into a powerful learning opportunity. This approach fosters both personal and professional development.

Practicing gratitude plays a crucial role in building emotional strength. By focusing on the positive aspects of life, gratitude reduces stress and enhances well-being. This shift in perspective not only improves mood but also nurtures a resilient outlook. Gratitude journals, where daily acknowledgments of things, people, or moments we are thankful for are recorded, serve as simple yet effective tools. They help embed a habit of positive thinking into daily routines, gradually leading to a more grateful and resilient mindset.

Mindfulness practices further contribute to resilience by enhancing awareness and reducing stress. Living in the present moment, mindfulness involves paying attention to one's thoughts and surroundings without judgment. This practice encourages emotional regulation and increases concentration, which builds mental clarity and focus—two essential components of resilience.

A practical example of mindfulness is incorporating mindful breathing exercises into your day. Taking a few minutes to focus solely on breath can significantly reduce stress levels. Apps like Headspace or Calm can aid in establishing this routine, providing structured guidance to cultivate a more mindful existence.

Building optimism is another key strategy in fostering resilience through a proactive and empowered mindset. Optimism involves reframing challenges as opportunities for growth and understanding that setbacks are temporary. This shift in thinking supports emotional stability and promotes a more hopeful outlook.

Throughout history, numerous successful individuals have demonstrated the power of optimism. J.K. Rowling, for example, faced multiple rejections before publishing the Harry Potter series. Her optimistic belief in her work and ability to see failure as part of the journey illustrates how reframing adversity can lead to significant achievements. Such real-world examples underscore the substantial benefits of maintaining a positive and optimistic attitude.

Additionally, engaging in activities that reinforce positive thinking is essential. Surrounding yourself with supportive, uplifting people helps create an environment conducive to resilience. Choosing to engage in conversations that inspire rather than drain energy bolsters emotional health. Social media can be a useful tool here; curating feeds to include motivational and growth-oriented content can continuously feed optimism and positive thought patterns.

Introducing small changes in how challenges and setbacks are perceived is a cornerstone of building lasting resilience. Viewing failures as learning experiences rather than final verdicts allows for continuous personal growth and confidence. This approach not only reinforces a growth mindset but also integrates an adaptable way of handling life's challenges.

Furthermore, it's important to acknowledge that many individuals may initially approach the idea of optimism and positive thinking with skepticism. Treating these strategies as experiments can alleviate such doubts. Keeping a journal to track progress and noting changes in mindset and resilience over time can provide tangible evidence of the benefits. These insights can validate the efforts and encourage continued practice.

Concluding Thoughts

In understanding how habits affect resilience, this chapter has explored the transformative power of establishing positive routines. By incorporating elements such as physical activity, mindfulness, and healthy eating into daily life, individuals can create a stable foundation to face challenges with greater ease. These empowering routines act as anchors in uncertain times, providing structure and predictability that mitigate stress and enhance emotional well-being. The intentional practice of reflection allows for deeper self-awareness, enabling the identification and modification of thought patterns that may hinder growth. As these habits become ingrained, they not only fortify mental strength but also encourage a mindset resilient to adversity.

Moreover, by breaking negative habitual patterns, individuals unlock their capacity for adaptability and emotional strength. Recognizing triggers and replacing detrimental behaviors with constructive activities fosters a healthier feedback loop, promoting lasting change. Accountability systems reinforce commitment and provide necessary support along this journey. The gradual establishment of new habits paves the way for sustainable behavior shifts, celebrating each small victory as a step towards larger goals. Through these efforts, one cultivates a resilient mindset capable of thriving amidst life's uncertainties, embracing challenges as opportunities for growth and transformation.

Chapter 8

Resilience in Everyday Life

R esilience in everyday life serves as a guiding force, helping individuals not just to withstand adversity, but to thrive amidst challenges. It is the inner strength that empowers us to bounce back from setbacks and adapt positively to changing situations, whether at home or in the workplace. Life's unpredictability can manifest in numerous forms, from stressful job environments to complex personal relationships. These experiences test our resilience, prompting us to draw on our emotional intelligence and problem-solving skills to navigate through turbulent times effectively. As we cultivate resilience, we discover an enhanced sense of control and stability that significantly contributes to our overall well-being and happiness.

This chapter delves into practical applications of resilience across different spheres of life. Readers will explore strategies for developing a resilient mindset in professional settings, including recognizing stressors and maintaining a balance between work and personal life. Insights into fostering supportive workplace relationships and developing emotional intelligence further amplify one's ability to handle work-related pressures. Moreover, the chapter extends into personal realms, offering techniques for nurturing relationships through effective communication, empathy, and managing conflicts constructively. These discussions aim to equip readers with actionable tools to strengthen their mental and emotional fortitude, enabling them to face life's ups and downs with unwavering resilience.

Adapting Resilience in the Workplace

Navigating workplace challenges requires a resilient mindset, enabling professionals to handle stress and adversity with confidence. A crucial step in cultivating resilience is recognizing stressors within the work environment. Understanding individual triggers and how they affect emotional well-being can empower employees to manage their reactions more effectively. Stressors could range from tight deadlines to interpersonal conflicts or even changes in job roles. By identifying these elements, individuals can better prepare for and respond to them without feeling overwhelmed. Taking time to reflect on past experiences and examining which factors contribute to one's stress levels can be an enlightening exercise, guiding future strategies to maintain calmness and control.

Developing a growth mindset is another powerful tool for incorporating resilience into professional life. This involves viewing feedback as a valuable opportunity for improvement rather than criticism and perceiving failures as lessons rather than setbacks. Embracing a growth mindset encourages employees to take risks and innovate without the fear of failure, fostering an environment where continuous learning is celebrated. For instance, when a project does not go as planned, instead of dwelling on its shortcomings, reflecting on what went wrong and how it can be rectified next time solidifies the foundation for personal and professional growth.

Maintaining a work-life balance plays a significant role in building resilience. Effectively managing time, setting clear boundaries between professional and personal life, and prioritizing self-care are essential practices. Time management can include scheduling breaks during the workday to recharge and assigning tasks wisely by prioritizing urgent and significant work over less critical activities. Work-life boundaries might mean disconnecting from work emails after hours to ensure personal space is respected. Self-care practices such as regular exercise, meditation, or hobbies provide necessary relaxation that enhances mental and emotional strength. An employee who invests in self-care is more equipped to face workplace challenges with a clear mind and positive attitude.

Furthermore, building supportive relationships with colleagues can enhance resilience by creating a network of mutual support and encouragement. Seeking mentorship offers invaluable insights and guidance based on experience, allowing mentees to navigate complex situations with increased confidence and understanding. Mentors can share their wisdom on handling various challenges, providing both practical advice and emotional reassurance. Additionally, engaging in team-building activities strengthens bonds among colleagues and cultivates a spirit of camaraderie and trust. Teamwork enables collective problem-solving and helps distribute the stress load, making challenges appear more manageable.

Collaborative environments foster resilience by promoting honest communication and shared goals. Open discussions about challenges and obstacles create opportunities for joint problem-solving and innovative solutions. Encouraging a culture where team members feel comfortable expressing concerns and sharing ideas helps reduce the stress associated with carrying burdens alone. When every member supports each other and contributes to the team's success, resilience becomes a collective trait that benefits the entire organization.

Emotional intelligence (EI) is pivotal in resilience, highlighting the importance of regulating emotions and practicing empathy at work. Recognizing and managing one's emotions, especially during stressful times, can prevent rash decisions and facilitate measured responses. Techniques like deep breathing or taking brief moments to refocus allow for thoughtful reactions instead of impulsive ones. Moreover, showing empathy towards others fosters a supportive workplace environment. Understanding coworkers' perspectives and emotions can help mitigate conflicts and strengthen team dynamics.

Leaders have a critical role in modeling resilience and encouraging it among their team. They can promote resilience-oriented practices by advocating for open communication, acknowledging employees' efforts, and supporting professional development. Providing constructive feedback and recognizing achievements nurtures a growth mindset and motivates employees to strive for excellence while embracing challenges. When leaders demonstrate resilience through their actions, it inspires their teams to adopt similar approaches in facing adversity.

Organizations can further support resilience through formalized training programs focused on developing mental, emotional, and behavioral skills to cope with workplace challenges. Resilience training can include exercises such as stress inoculation and mindfulness meditation, equipping employees with practical techniques to manage high-pressure situations. These programs can also focus on cognitive restructuring to shift negative thought patterns, bolstering employees' abilities to maintain positivity and perseverance amid difficulties.

Resilience in Personal Relationships

Resilience plays an undeniably crucial role in nurturing personal connections, allowing relationships to thrive even in the face of adversity. One significant aspect of resilience in relationships is effective communication. Communication is the lifeline that keeps any relationship healthy and robust. Practicing honest dialogue requires more than just speaking your mind; it involves expressing thoughts and feelings genuinely and transparently. This openness fosters trust and understanding, which are the pillars of a resilient relationship.

In addition to being forthright, vulnerability is essential. Being vulnerable means sharing your innermost feelings, fears, and desires with your partner, requiring courage and trust. Vulnerability breeds closeness and compassion, reinforcing the bond between individuals. It's about lowering defenses and allowing the other person into your emotional world, creating a shared space of mutual respect.

Active listening is equally fundamental in effective communication. It's not merely hearing words but understanding the emotions and intentions behind them. When people feel truly heard, they experience validation and support, key elements in building resilience. Practice patience and attentiveness while listening; give your full attention to the speaker, avoiding the urge to interrupt or rush to solutions. This practice can lead to insightful conversations where both partners feel valued and understood.

Managing conflict constructively is another cornerstone of resilience in relationships. Conflicts are inevitable, but handling them with a solution-oriented mindset transforms potential barriers into opportunities for growth. Instead of viewing conflicts as threats, consider them chances to understand differing perspectives and collaborate on mutually beneficial solutions.

A respectful disagreement is key; this means acknowledging differences without belittling or dismissing the other party's views. Approach discussions with the intention of understanding rather than merely winning. Using "I" statements instead of "you" statements helps articulate personal feelings and experiences without placing blame. For example, saying "I feel upset when plans change unexpectedly" focuses on personal feelings rather than accusing the partner, fostering a more constructive dialogue (Otting, 2024).

To further strengthen personal connections, cultivating empathy is invaluable. Empathy involves understanding and sharing the feelings of others. It goes beyond sympathy by actively engaging with loved ones' emotional needs. By providing empathetic responses, you validate their experiences, instilling comfort and reassurance. Recognize that everyone has distinct emotional landscapes; taking time to explore these landscapes can deepen your connection, promoting a resilient bond.

Additionally, resilience in relationships thrives on the commitment to grow together. Engaging in shared activities not only provides entertainment but also strengthens the partnership by offering avenues for collaboration, trust-building, and shared memories. These activities can range from simple walks or cooking meals together to tackling projects or traveling, each presenting unique challenges and rewards.

Supporting each other's personal development is equally imperative. Encourage your partner's aspirations and provide moral support during tough times, reinforcing the partnership. Celebrating each other's achievements fosters an environment of positivity and mutual encouragement, vital for sustaining resilience through life's ups and downs.

Implementing guidelines for managing conflict and communication serves as an actionable roadmap. Start with open dialogues; ensure both parties feel safe expressing themselves without fear of judgment or repercussions. Develop active listening skills by maintaining eye contact, nodding in acknowledgment, and asking clarifying questions to demonstrate engagement (Center, 2023).

When disagreements arise, use "I" statements to express how you feel without attributing blame. For instance, "I feel hurt when..." allows for personal expression without inciting defensiveness. Lastly, approach every conflict with the aim of resolution rather than victory; seek common ground and propose compromises that satisfy both parties.

Integrating Resilience Strategies across Life Domains

Resilience is a skill that, when applied across various aspects of life, can significantly enhance adaptability and overall well-being. To effectively harness resilience, it's crucial to first identify and manage stressors in different environments. Stress can sneak up on us from numerous angles—workplace pressures, personal relationships, or unexpected life changes. Recognizing these stressors is the first step towards developing proactive coping techniques. By acknowledging what triggers stress, individuals can start building personalized strategies to tackle them head-on. This might include deep-breathing exercises during tense moments or setting aside time to reflect and strategize on how best to navigate challenges. Understanding these stressors empowers people to remain calm and composed, even in the face of adversity (7 Steps to Manage Stress and Build Resilience | Office of Research on Women's Health, n.d.).

A continuous learning approach plays a vital role in applying resilience. Embracing challenges and setbacks not as failures but as opportunities for growth is key. Continuous learning fosters a mindset where setbacks are stepping stones rather than stumbling blocks. When faced with a challenging project at work or a personal disappointment, viewing these situations as learning experiences can transform how they are perceived. Instead of seeing difficulties as roadblocks, envision them as new paths to explore, full of potential lessons. Take the example of an employee who misses out on a promotion. By seeking feedback and additional training, they not only improve their skills but may also prepare themselves better for future opportunities. Adopting this mindset encourages adaptability and fosters a stronger, more resilient character (McQuillen, 2024).

Equally important is the establishment of healthy boundaries and prioritization of self-care to sustain emotional health and productivity. In today's fast-paced world, the lines between personal and professional life often blur, leading to burnout and stress. Setting clear boundaries ensures that there is time dedicated solely to rest and recharge. It involves knowing when to say no to a meeting that encroaches upon personal time or ensuring that there is ample space for activities that rejuvenate the mind and body. Self-care practices like regular exercise, meditation, and pursuing hobbies can provide necessary respite, allowing for more balanced and productive living.

These habits are essential not just for mental and emotional wellness, but also for maintaining peak performance in daily tasks (7 Steps to Manage Stress and Build Resilience | Office of Research on Women's Health, n.d.).

Moreover, nurturing supportive networks both personally and professionally significantly enhances resilience. Humans are inherently social beings, and having a robust support system provides a safety net during tough times. Whether it's leaning on friends and family for emotional support or collaborating with colleagues to brainstorm solutions, these connections offer a sense of belonging and reassurance. Building these networks requires effort and intentionality, such as initiating meaningful conversations, participating actively in community or professional groups, and being open to seeking help when necessary. A strong network acts as a pillar, offering support through shared experiences and collective wisdom, which is invaluable for fostering resilience (7 Steps to Manage Stress and Build Resilience | Office of Research on Women's Health, n.d.).

Each of these strategies—managing stressors, embracing continuous learning, establishing boundaries for self-care, and nurturing support networks—contributes to building a resilient foundation. While adopting these strategies, remember that resilience is a journey, not a destination. It evolves with each experience and adapts to changing circumstances. Therefore, consistently applying these strategies across various domains of life can lead to enhanced adaptability and well-being.

Final Insights

In this chapter, we've explored the essential role that resilience plays in both personal and professional domains. We delved into techniques for recognizing stressors and how understanding these triggers can empower individuals to manage their reactions and maintain control during challenging situations. Embracing a growth mindset emerged as a valuable approach, encouraging professionals to view setbacks as learning opportunities rather than failures. This mindset fosters an environment where learning is continuous, paving the way for innovation and confidence. By setting clear boundaries between work and personal life, prioritizing self-care, and nurturing supportive relationships, individuals can build a resilient foundation that helps them thrive even in high-stress environments.

Moreover, we emphasized the importance of effective communication and empathy in personal relationships, highlighting how these elements contribute to lasting connections. Practicing active listening, managing conflicts constructively, and fostering a commitment to grow together all nurture resilience within partnerships. Whether it's through shared activities or supporting each other's aspirations, these practices reinforce emotional bonds and adaptability. As we conclude this chapter, remember that resilience is a journey that evolves with experiences. By continuously applying these strategies across various aspects of life, you can enhance your adaptability and well-being, equipping yourself to face life's challenges with optimism and strength.

Chapter 9

Learning from Failure

L earning from failure is a pivotal life skill that transforms setbacks into opportunities for growth. While society often prizes success and achievement, it is through our missteps and errors that we often learn the most profound lessons. This chapter invites you to shift your perspective on failure, viewing it not as an end but as an integral component of a broader journey toward personal and professional fulfillment. By understanding how each failure harbors valuable insights, readers can begin to see adversity as a catalyst for innovation and self-discovery.

In this chapter, we will explore the ways in which individuals can harness their setbacks to forge new paths to success. You'll gain practical insights into dissecting failures objectively, identifying areas for improvement, and creating action plans that prioritize small, achievable goals. The chapter also covers the importance of cultivating resilience—a mindset that enables you to face adversity with courage and determination. Through examining stories of renowned individuals who have triumphed over challenges, along with strategies to bolster emotional and mental well-being, you'll be equipped to transform failures into stepping stones for future achievements.

Failure as a Learning Tool

Failure is an inevitable part of life and learning. It serves as a critical teacher, with lessons that can forge personal and professional growth. Understanding failure requires a shift in perspective. Instead of seeing mistakes as definitive losses, we should view them as stepping stones to success. Embracing this notion encourages us to accept imperfections not as endpoints but as opportunities to learn and evolve.

Acknowledging failure isn't simply about accepting defeat. It's about harnessing the potential each setback brings for self-improvement. Every failure presents a chance to analyze what went wrong. This analysis helps identify areas for improvement, enabling us to make informed decisions in the future. By dissecting our missteps, we uncover insights into our habits, choices, and strategies that might contribute to negative outcomes. This analysis approach is crucial because it forms the foundation upon which future success is built (Emanuele, 2020).

Analyzing failures involves assessing the situation objectively. Take a step back from the emotional impact and look at the facts. Was it a lack of preparation? Did external factors play a larger role than anticipated? Being honest with ourselves is key. By doing so, we can map out a clearer path forward, steering ourselves away from previously encountered pitfalls (Emanuele, 2020). It's this diligent introspection that lays the groundwork for making better decisions in future endeavors.

Beyond analysis lies the development of skills to extract essential lessons from past experiences. Each failure provides unique information that can be applied to new situations. Developing these skills requires active engagement with our past encounters. Reflect on how certain decisions led to specific outcomes, and explore alternative actions that could have been taken instead. By doing so, we cultivate a sharper intuition for navigating similar challenges.

This skill-building process extends beyond simply preventing past mistakes. It encompasses the ability to adapt, innovate, and respond creatively when faced with adversity. Those who learn to see failures as mere detours, rather than dead-ends, often find themselves on pathways they hadn't considered before. These detours lead to innovative solutions and new opportunities that fuel further growth.

Central to transforming failure into valuable lessons is cultivating a mindset anchored in resilience and persistence. Resilience doesn't mean avoiding failure; it means facing it with courage and determination, understanding that setbacks are not only expected but beneficial. Persistence fuels the drive to keep moving forward despite obstacles. It is the fortitude to rise after every fall, armed with the knowledge gained from previous attempts (Turning Failures into Opportunities for Growth and Success with Resilience, 2022).

A resilient mindset also involves maintaining a positive outlook on the future while being realistic about current challenges. It's about balancing optimism with practicality, acknowledging that the path to success will be riddled with hurdles but believing wholeheartedly in our capacity to overcome them. It's easy to feel discouraged after repeated failures, yet resilient individuals recognize that each attempt brings them closer to success. They thrive on the idea that perseverance, combined with learned insights, will eventually yield rewards.

To foster resilience, it's important to nurture supportive relationships and focus on personal well-being. Friends, family, and colleagues can provide encouragement and different perspectives during difficult times. Emotional support bolsters our ability to manage stress and maintain a balanced approach to problem-solving.

Furthermore, taking care of one's mental, physical, and emotional health enhances resilience. Engaging in wellness activities such as exercise, meditation, and mindfulness strengthens our coping mechanisms. This holistic approach prepares us to face challenges with clarity and composure, ready to turn any failure into a constructive lesson.

Turning Defeat into Motivation

In a world that celebrates success and achievement, setbacks can often feel like daunting roadblocks. However, changing our perspective on these obstacles can transform them into powerful motivators for growth and progress. Recognizing defeat as a motivational force allows us to ignite new passions and inspire determination in ways we might not have imagined.

Instead of seeing failure as a conclusion, think of it as the beginning of a new chapter filled with opportunities. When faced with setbacks, allow them to fuel your drive toward discovering what truly excites and inspires you. This renewed passion can become an engine for creativity, pushing you toward uncharted territories where innovation thrives. For instance, many successful entrepreneurs credit their failures as the catalyst for new ideas that eventually led to groundbreaking innovations.

To navigate through setbacks effectively, it's vital to establish an action plan that includes realistic short-term targets. These targets serve as stepping stones, providing a sense of direction and accomplishment that rebuilds confidence and momentum along the way. Instead of aiming only for end goals, breaking down challenges into smaller, manageable tasks can make the journey less overwhelming. Achieving these interim milestones reinforces a sense of capability and establishes a pattern of success.

In setting these realistic goals, remember the broader picture but focus on achievable steps. This approach ensures that once a setback is encountered, you're better equipped to tackle it without being solely fixated on a potentially distant destination. Adapting your action plan as circumstances evolve aligns with maintaining flexibility and resilience—a practice essential for overcoming adversity. This agile mindset aligns with the strategic "push, push, pause" approach described by Dagenais (2024), which emphasizes adaptability over rigidity.

Another crucial element in harnessing setbacks for personal development is the use of positive affirmations. In times of challenge, our thoughts can significantly influence our emotional resilience. Positive affirmations help create a mental framework that encourages resilience and optimism. By consciously repeating affirmations like "I am capable," or "Every setback is a setup for a comeback," individuals can cultivate a hopeful outlook even during trying times. This reinforcement of self-belief can gradually shift perspectives, allowing one's inner strength to shine through the shadows of doubt.

Moreover, surrounding yourself with supportive individuals plays a pivotal role in overcoming setbacks. Friends, family, mentors, and colleagues who offer encouragement can be instrumental in navigating tough patches. The presence of a support network not only provides emotional backing but also offers diverse perspectives and advice that can bring solutions to light. Trusted individuals can serve as sounding boards, helping you view setbacks from different angles and reducing feelings of isolation.

The influence of community cannot be overstated when seeking motivation after setbacks. Being part of a supportive network opens avenues for collaboration, learning, and sharing experiences. Hearing how others have triumphed over similar adversities can rekindle hope and determination. Moreover, this communal encouragement instills a sense of accountability that drives you to persevere.

Ultimately, using setbacks as catalysts for progress involves embracing change and nurturing the belief that growth stems from adversity. By shifting focus from the fear of failure to its potential for inspiration and transformation, you can harness setbacks as springboards into realms of greater achievement.

Setting New Goals

In the journey toward success, setbacks are inevitable. They might seem daunting at first, yet hold the hidden potential to guide us toward a path of renewed purpose and innovation. Redefining objectives after experiencing failure is a critical step in turning setbacks into stepping stones for future achievements.

When confronted with failure, the initial reaction might be discouragement or self-doubt. However, it's important to view this as an opportunity for reassessment. Reassessing goals does not imply abandoning them; rather, it involves taking a moment to reflect on what could be improved or changed. This process starts with an honest evaluation of what went wrong and why. Was the goal too ambitious? Were the strategies employed ineffective? By addressing these questions, we gain valuable insights into the areas that need adjustment.

Setting achievable milestones becomes crucial in regaining momentum and focus. After failure, breaking down larger goals into smaller, manageable steps can reignite motivation. These milestones act as checkpoints, allowing us to celebrate small victories along the way. This approach not only prevents overwhelm but also helps maintain a sense of progress. Each milestone achieved serves as a building block towards the ultimate goal, reinforcing our commitment and resilience.

Adapting goals in response to setbacks can lead to innovative solutions and foster a renewed sense of purpose. When faced with obstacles, it's worthwhile to explore alternative approaches that may not have been considered initially. The ability to pivot and adjust plans is often where innovation thrives. By adopting a flexible mindset, we open ourselves up to creative problem-solving and new opportunities that were previously unimagined. This adaptability not only enhances our chances of success but also instills a deeper understanding of our own capabilities and strengths.

Stories of successful individuals who have triumphed over repeated failures offer profound lessons and inspiration. Thomas Edison, for example, famously failed thousands of times before inventing the light bulb. His persistence and unwavering belief in his vision remind us that failure is not the end but merely a stepping stone to greatness. Similarly, J.K. Rowling faced numerous rejections before publishing the Harry Potter series, which has since become a global phenomenon. These stories illustrate the power of perseverance and the importance of redefining objectives in the face of adversity.

Successful people often share common traits: resilience, determination, and a willingness to learn from their mistakes. Emulating these qualities can help us navigate our own challenges with grace and tenacity. It's essential to remember that failure does not define us; rather, how we respond to it does. Viewing setbacks as temporary detours rather than permanent roadblocks empowers us to keep moving forward with renewed vigor.

Creating an action plan that incorporates realistic short-term targets can further reinforce these principles. This structured approach ensures that we remain focused and motivated, even when the outcome seems uncertain.

Regularly reviewing and adjusting this plan allows us to stay aligned with our evolving goals and objectives.

It's worth noting the importance of celebrating effort alongside progress. Acknowledging the hard work and dedication invested in pursuing our goals not only boosts morale but also strengthens our resolve to continue. Recognizing these efforts serves as a reminder that growth is a continuous journey, marked by both successes and failures.

Final Insights

Reflecting on this chapter, we've explored how setbacks, rather than being seen as defeats, can serve as valuable tools for learning and growth. The insights gained from failures provide an opportunity to reassess our goals and strategies, enabling us to make more informed decisions in the future. By examining what went wrong and why, we uncover crucial lessons that enhance our ability to adapt and innovate. This approach encourages not only the development of new skills but also nurtures a mindset grounded in resilience and persistence. Through embracing these experiences, we learn that each setback is not an end but a stepping stone towards success.

As we navigate through life's challenges, it's important to maintain a positive outlook while being realistic about the hurdles we may face. A strong support network and focus on personal well-being further bolster our resilience, helping us manage stress and maintain clarity during difficult times. By aligning our action plans with achievable milestones, we build confidence and momentum, turning each small victory into a building block for larger achievements. Ultimately, by viewing setbacks as opportunities for motivation and transformation, we harness their power to propel us into realms of greater accomplishment and personal growth.

Chapter 10

Emotional Intelligence and Resilience

E motional intelligence is an invaluable asset in navigating life's challenges, offering insights into how we perceive and manage our emotions. It is the compass that guides us through uncertain waters, allowing us to understand ourselves and others more profoundly. As we explore the intricate relationship between emotional intelligence and resilience, we uncover how these skills not only support personal growth but also fortify our ability to bounce back from adversity. This journey invites us to delve deeper into our emotional landscapes, unveiling the potential for transformation and empowerment hidden within.

In this chapter, you will discover the importance of recognizing emotional triggers and how they influence our responses to stress and adversity. We will explore practical strategies like journaling and mindfulness that can help identify and manage these triggers, enhancing self-awareness and emotional regulation. Additionally, we'll discuss the role of empathy in strengthening resilience by fostering deeper connections and understanding with others. Through active listening and empathy exercises, you'll learn how to build supportive relationships that serve as pillars of strength during challenging times. Furthermore, we will introduce proactive coping strategies and techniques for enhancing emotional regulation, equipping you with tools to manage stress effectively. By integrating these practices into daily life, you will not only bolster your emotional intelligence but also cultivate a resilient mindset capable of thriving amidst life's trials.

Recognizing Emotional Triggers

Understanding and managing emotional triggers is a crucial aspect of building resilience. Emotional triggers are specific situations or stimuli that provoke intense emotional responses. By recognizing these triggers, we can develop the ability to respond more thoughtfully and constructively, enhancing our resilience in challenging situations.

The first step in this journey is identifying common emotional triggers. Triggers often stem from past experiences, unresolved issues, or particular scenarios that evoke strong reactions. For instance, a critical comment at work might remind someone of past criticisms, leading to an exaggerated response. Understanding what situations provoke emotional responses allows us to anticipate and better manage them.

A practical way to identify triggers is through journaling, a powerful tool for tracking and revealing patterns in emotional reactions. By recording daily experiences and noting any strong emotions that arise, individuals can gain insights into recurring themes or situations that consistently trigger certain emotions. Journaling fosters self-awareness, making it easier to predict and prepare for emotional challenges. For example, someone might notice they feel anxious in meetings where opinions are openly debated, highlighting a potential area for personal growth (Godreau, 2024).

Mindfulness techniques play a significant role in managing emotional triggers by helping individuals remain present and aware of their feelings without being overwhelmed by them. Mindfulness involves paying attention to one's thoughts, emotions, and sensations in the moment. This practice allows individuals to observe their emotional responses with curiosity rather than judgment, enabling them to respond rather than react impulsively. Simple mindfulness exercises, such as focused breathing or body scans, can be incorporated into daily routines to build emotional resilience over time (Cooks-Campbell, 2022).

Furthermore, developing action plans for coping with identified triggers is essential in reducing anxiety and strengthening resilience. Once triggers are known, creating strategies to address them can help mitigate their impact. These strategies might include setting boundaries in potentially triggering situations, practicing assertive communication, or having a list of calming activities to engage in when feeling overwhelmed. By having a plan in place, individuals can approach emotionally challenging situations with confidence and clarity, knowing they are equipped to handle them effectively.

It's also beneficial to seek guidance from mental health professionals during this process. Therapists and counselors are skilled at helping individuals explore the roots of their triggers and develop personalized coping strategies. They can provide valuable insights and tools, such as cognitive-behavioral techniques, that encourage constructive thought patterns and behaviors. In some cases, exploring deeper issues through therapeutic modalities like Eye Movement Desensitization and Reprocessing (EMDR) therapy may be beneficial, particularly for those dealing with trauma-related triggers.

While understanding emotional triggers, it's important to recognize that resilience is not about avoiding difficult emotions but learning to navigate and recover from them constructively. This perspective encourages a growth mindset, where challenges are viewed as opportunities for personal development. With continued effort, individuals can transform their relationship with their triggers, ultimately fostering greater emotional intelligence and resilience.

Developing Empathy

Cultivating empathy is essential for building resilience and improving personal and professional relationships. It involves understanding others' perspectives, which enriches relationships and fosters compassion. By seeing the world through someone else's eyes, we create deeper connections that last.

Understanding others' perspectives can transform how we interact with peers, family, and colleagues. It helps us break down barriers and dispel misunderstandings, allowing for genuine dialogues and stronger bonds. For example, considering a colleague's point of view during a project dispute can help find common ground and develop effective solutions together. This form of empathy does more than improve individual relationships; it encourages a culture of openness and cooperation, ultimately enhancing collective resilience in groups or teams.

Active listening skills are vital in fostering empathetic responses and building trust. When we listen actively, we demonstrate genuine interest in the speaker's thoughts and feelings, encouraging them to share more openly. Active listening involves focusing entirely on the speaker, refraining from interrupting, and responding thoughtfully. This not only builds rapport but also strengthens trust. In a work environment, active listening can de-escalate conflicts and foster a supportive atmosphere, making it easier for all parties involved to adapt to challenges with greater resilience.

One practical guideline to enhance active listening is to focus on non-verbal cues, such as facial expressions and body language. These subtle signals often convey more than words and provide insights into the speaker's emotions and concerns. Reflecting back what has been heard or asking clarifying questions shows attentiveness and validates the speaker's experience, further building empathy and trust (How to Be More Empathetic: 8 Exercises to Develop Empathy — Calm Blog, n.d.).

Engaging in empathy exercises, like role-playing, can significantly improve responses to diverse scenarios. Role-playing allows individuals to step into another person's shoes, providing insights that lead to deeper understanding and empathy. For instance, a manager could role-play the perspective of an employee facing personal challenges, gaining better appreciation for their situation and adjusting support strategies accordingly. Such exercises are not just about developing empathy but also building resilience by enabling individuals to navigate complex interactions thoughtfully and considerately.

Role-playing is an excellent way to practice empathy because it removes us from our comfort zones, challenging us to approach situations with humility and open-mindedness. It encourages us to confront biases and preconceptions, promoting growth and understanding (Sutton, 2020). As we become more adept at perceiving and respecting differing viewpoints, we evolve into more compassionate and resilient individuals.

Building a supportive network of empathetic individuals is crucial for nurturing a robust emotional support system. Surrounding ourselves with empathy-rich environments provides a secure foundation where we can share experiences, seek guidance, and gain encouragement. This network becomes a safety net during times of stress or adversity, offering reassurance and fostering resilience. A community of empathetic people supports each other emotionally, reinforcing positive coping mechanisms and fortifying mental health.

To cultivate such networks, it is beneficial to engage regularly with people who exhibit empathy and understanding. Participating in group activities, volunteering, or joining support groups offers opportunities to connect with like-minded individuals. Sharing stories and experiences helps build mutual trust and encourages group cohesion, creating a shared sense of purpose and resilience. An empathetic support network not only enhances personal well-being but also contributes to the resilience and strength of the entire community (Miller, 2019).

In both personal and professional spheres, empathy acts as the glue that binds us together. By understanding others deeply, listening actively, engaging in empathy-building exercises, and establishing strong support networks, we elevate our capacity for endurance and adaptation in the face of life's challenges. Resilience flourishes when individuals feel understood and supported, creating a fertile ground for emotional growth and collaborative success.

Developing these empathetic skills requires conscious effort and commitment but yields significant rewards in terms of emotional intelligence and resilience. The journey towards cultivating empathy is ongoing, marked by small, meaningful interactions that gradually transform our relationships and fortify our inner strength. Whether facing day-to-day stressors or major life adversities, empathetic connections ensure we are never alone in our struggles, enabling us to rise above difficulties with grace and courage.

Emotional Regulation Techniques

Enhancing one's emotional regulation is a cornerstone of effective stress management. The interplay between emotional intelligence and resilience becomes crucial in today's fast-paced world, where stress can often feel overwhelming. To navigate this, the practice of mindfulness emerges as a vital tool. By engaging in mindfulness, individuals can cultivate a sense of clarity and balance during emotional upheavals. This ancient technique involves paying attention to the present moment with openness and non-judgment, helping to anchor emotions that might otherwise spiral out of control.

Incorporating mindfulness into daily routines allows for a deeper awareness of emotions, acting as a buffer against the chaos of stress. Regular mindfulness practice not only aids in recognizing what triggers certain emotions but also provides the space to choose more adaptive responses rather than being swept away by reactive impulses. Through this process, individuals learn to return to a state of equilibrium, enhancing their ability to manage stress effectively (Scott, 2022).

Reflection and journaling are additional practices that can significantly enhance one's ability to regulate emotions. By setting aside time to reflect on experiences and emotions through journaling, individuals can begin to identify and track recurring themes in their emotional responses. This act of writing down thoughts and feelings enables one to prioritize problems, fears, and concerns, thus offering a clearer perspective on how to manage them. Journaling serves as a repository of personal insights and emotional patterns, providing an opportunity for positive self-talk and identifying negative thought patterns (University of Rochester Medical Center, 2019).

By keeping a journal, one can track day-to-day symptoms, recognize triggers, and learn strategies to better control them. This leads to increased self-awareness, making it easier to implement targeted management strategies for emotional regulation. For instance, if stress consistently peaks at certain times or situations, journaling helps in formulating a plan to address these specific instances proactively, reducing their impact. Moreover, it acts as a tool for brainstorming solutions, empowering individuals to face challenges with structured responses rather than feeling overwhelmed.

Proactive coping strategies are essential when anticipating potential stressors. These strategies help individuals develop a framework to handle future challenges before they arise. By planning ahead, one can create structured responses tailored to likely scenarios, reducing the uncertainty that often accompanies stressful events. This anticipation not only minimizes stress but also builds confidence in one's ability to handle unexpected situations calmly and effectively.

An important aspect of proactive coping is building flexibility into one's plans, allowing for adjustments as circumstances change. By doing so, individuals maintain a sense of control and adaptability, which are critical components of resilience. Implementing proactive strategies requires practice and mindfulness— understanding past emotional reactions and crafting new approaches to similar stressors. In this way, decision-making becomes more reflective, supporting healthier emotional outcomes over time.

Personal emotional awareness is another vital component in strengthening emotional regulation. By becoming attuned to personal emotional triggers and patterns, individuals gain insight into how their emotions influence behavior. This self-awareness lays the foundation for self-regulation, guiding individuals towards more adaptive behaviors in challenging situations. Identifying personal patterns involves observing how emotions manifest physically and behaviorally. This awareness transforms automatic reactions into deliberate choices, promoting resilience in the face of adversity.

Through this self-awareness, people can recognize when they are veering toward emotionally reactive states and deploy techniques such as deep breathing, reflection, or a brief pause, to recalibrate. Understanding that emotions are not fixed but can be managed and redirected fosters a growth mindset and empowers individuals to transform stress into opportunities for learning and development.

Final Thoughts

In this chapter, we explored the profound link between emotional intelligence and resilience by delving into techniques that enhance our emotional well-being. Recognizing and managing emotional triggers is a vital first step, as it empowers us to respond thoughtfully rather than reacting impulsively. Through practices like journaling and mindfulness, individuals can identify patterns in their emotional responses and develop strategies for handling them with greater poise. These small yet significant actions build the foundation for navigating life's challenges with confidence, turning potential stressors into stepping stones for growth.

Furthermore, empathy and emotional regulation emerge as crucial contributors to resilience. By understanding others' perspectives and actively listening, we foster stronger connections that provide emotional support during tough times. Practicing empathy not only strengthens relationships but also enriches our ability to adapt to adversity. Additionally, emotional regulation techniques, such as proactive coping strategies and personal emotional awareness, equip us to face stress head-on. Through these insights and practices, readers are encouraged to embrace their emotional journeys, transforming difficult experiences into opportunities for learning and resilience.

Chapter 11

Mindfulness and Stress Reduction

M indfulness and stress reduction are intertwined concepts that invite us to explore the depths of our consciousness and discover new avenues for personal growth and emotional resilience. As we embark on this journey, it becomes evident how cultivating mindfulness can transform our relationship with stress, guiding us toward a more harmonious existence. By embracing this practice, we not only learn to navigate life's challenges with grace but also uncover the hidden potential within ourselves to withstand adversity. The path to mindfulness is as enriching as it is enlightening, promising to reshape our mental state in ways that foster tranquility and strength.

In this chapter, readers will delve into various mindfulness practices that serve as practical tools for reducing stress and enhancing resilience. Through these practices, individuals can attain a heightened sense of awareness and clarity, which are essential for effective stress management. Techniques such as meditation, deep breathing exercises, mindful walking, and body scans will be explored in detail, each offering unique benefits for cultivating emotional stability and mental fortitude. Readers will discover how these methods can be seamlessly integrated into daily routines, providing not only immediate relief from stress but also long-term resilience. By understanding and applying these techniques, individuals will gain the skills necessary to respond to stress thoughtfully, rather than react impulsively, thereby enriching their personal and professional lives. Ultimately, this chapter aims to equip readers with the knowledge and tools needed to harness the power of mindfulness, empowering them to lead more balanced and fulfilling lives amidst the stresses of modern living.

Practices of Mindfulness

Mindfulness practices are powerful tools that can help foster resilience and enhance mental clarity in our lives. At the heart of many mindfulness techniques is meditation, a practice that anchors our thoughts in the present moment, reducing anxiety and serving as a reliable tool for stress reduction (Mayo Clinic Staff, 2022). For those who find themselves overwhelmed by worries about the future or ruminations on the past, meditation offers a reprieve. It helps create a space where one can observe thoughts without judgment, allowing feelings to pass naturally without gripping onto them.

A practical approach to meditation involves sitting comfortably with a straight back, feet planted firmly on the ground, and hands resting in your lap. The focus is primarily on the breath — observing how it flows in and out of your body. This simple act of awareness pulls you into the here and now, grounding you. As thoughts inevitably arise, they should be acknowledged without engagement, guiding attention gently back to the breath each time. This discipline not only quiets the mind but builds emotional resilience, preparing individuals to face challenges with calmness and clarity. Over time, this practice bolsters an individual's ability to respond to stress rather than react impulsively, cultivating a balanced mindset.

In addition to meditation, deep breathing exercises play a vital role in activating the body's relaxation response. These exercises involve intentional breathing patterns that shift focus and lessen the hold stressors have over us. Deep breathing acts as a reset button, helping us tap into inner reserves of calm and enhancing our emotional resilience (Ackerman, 2017). When we concentrate on the rhythm of our breath, filling our lungs deeply and exhaling fully, we engage the parasympathetic nervous system. This physiological response counteracts the fight-or-flight response that stress triggers. By incorporating these exercises regularly into daily life, greater control over emotions is achieved, leading to improved stress management.

When feeling tense or anxious, take a moment to pause. Begin by inhaling deeply through the nose, letting the air fill your abdomen, then slowly exhale through the mouth. Repeat this cycle for several minutes. Notice how deliberately shifting your breathing pattern can guide your mind away from the loop of negative thoughts and into a realm of tranquility. This practice not only alleviates immediate stress but also builds a foundation of emotional stability and resilience over time.

Mindful walking offers another effective method for integrating mindfulness into everyday life. This practice combines physical movement with mindful awareness, creating an opportunity to connect with the environment and oneself deeply. Unlike traditional walking, mindful walking emphasizes being present in each step, noticing the sensations in the soles of your feet, the rhythm of your strides, and the movement of your body and arms. Mindful walking can be incorporated into daily routines effortlessly, whether it's during a short break at work or a leisurely stroll at home. Find a quiet space, free from distractions, to walk a few meters back and forth while maintaining steady awareness of each motion. This practice encourages a sense of presence, making it easier to carry mindfulness into other areas of life while promoting peace of mind, which fortifies resilience against stress.

The body scan is another mindfulness technique that promotes self-awareness and reduces stress. During a body scan, participants focus their attention on different parts of their body, from head to toe, noting any sensations, tensions, or discomfort without judgment. This practice cultivates self-acceptance and reinforces a connection between mind and body, helping to release physical tension associated with stress (Mayo Clinic Staff, 2022). To perform a body scan, find a comfortable position lying down. Start with your toes and progressively move upwards, acknowledging how each area feels. Is there warmth, coolness, tingling, or heaviness? Instead of attempting to change anything, simply observe and accept.

By fostering awareness of bodily sensations without attachment, individuals learn to recognize how stress manifests physically. This recognition aids in addressing stress proactively, enabling better control over reactions to external pressures. Routine practice of the body scan can make one more attuned to their body's needs and responses, ultimately contributing to greater emotional and physical resilience.

Mindfulness in Stress Management

Mindfulness serves as a powerful coping mechanism for stress, offering practical methods that can be seamlessly incorporated into daily routines to enhance resilience and well-being. One of the fundamental aspects of mindfulness is its ability to help individuals recognize stress signals early on. By fostering an awareness of these signals, mindfulness empowers individuals to respond proactively, preventing stress from escalating into overwhelming situations.

Recognizing stress signals involves tuning in to one's thoughts, emotions, and bodily sensations without judgment. This increased awareness allows individuals to identify when they are beginning to feel tense or anxious, providing an opportunity to address these feelings before they intensify. For instance, someone might notice a tightening in their shoulders or a quickening of their breath during a stressful meeting. With mindfulness, this recognition becomes a cue to take a few deep breaths, ground oneself in the present moment, and approach the situation with a clear and calm mind. This proactive response not only helps in managing immediate stress but also builds long-term resilience by reinforcing positive coping strategies (Zandi et al., 2021).

Moreover, mindfulness encourages thoughtful responses rather than impulsive reactions, fostering balanced decision-making. In high-stress environments, it's easy to fall into automatic patterns of behavior that may not serve us well. Mindfulness interrupts this cycle by creating a space between stimulus and response. By practicing mindfulness, individuals learn to pause and consider their options rather than reacting impulsively.

This pause allows them to engage their "wise mind," as described in mindfulness literature, leading to more measured and effective decision-making processes (How to Manage Stress with Mindfulness and Meditation, 2021).

For example, consider a scenario where a project deadline is looming, and tension is rising among team members. A mindful individual would take a moment to breathe and center themselves before responding to a colleague's criticism or suggestion. This approach not only mitigates potential conflict but also promotes a collaborative atmosphere, enhancing productivity and reducing stress for everyone involved. By cultivating mindfulness, individuals develop greater emotional intelligence, allowing them to navigate challenging interactions with empathy and understanding.

Incorporating mindfulness into conflict resolution further highlights its practical applications. When faced with disagreements, mindfulness practices enable individuals to approach conflicts with an open and empathetic mindset. By being fully present during difficult conversations, one can listen actively and understand different perspectives, which fosters a more cooperative environment. This can significantly reduce tension and pave the way for effective collaboration and problem-solving.

Empathy plays a crucial role in resolving conflicts, helping parties involved feel heard and valued. Mindful communication emphasizes clarity and compassion, which can de-escalate potentially heated situations and lead to mutually beneficial outcomes. For professionals in high-stress jobs, developing these skills through mindfulness can greatly enhance workplace dynamics and improve overall job satisfaction. By prioritizing connection over confrontation, mindfulness nurtures a culture of respect and understanding, which is essential for maintaining healthy interpersonal relationships in both personal and professional contexts (Zandi et al., 2021).

Integrating mindfulness into a daily routine solidifies habits that effectively reduce stress and foster well-being. Consistency is key to reaping the benefits of mindfulness. Simple practices such as mindful breathing, guided meditation, or mindful walking can be incorporated into everyday life with minimal disruption. Setting aside even just a few minutes each day for mindfulness can make a substantial difference in managing stress levels over the long term.

Creating a routine that incorporates mindfulness encourages the development of positive habits. For example, starting the day with a brief meditation session can set a calm and focused tone for the hours ahead. Similarly, taking a mindful walk during lunch breaks provides an opportunity to reset and recharge before tackling afternoon tasks. These small, intentional practices accumulate over time, leading to a more resilient and centered approach to life's challenges.

To cultivate mindfulness effectively, establishing a dedicated time for mindful practices within one's daily schedule can be invaluable. Begin by choosing a quiet and comfortable space where distractions are minimized. Start with short sessions, gradually increasing the duration as familiarity with the practice grows. Focus on the breath, sensations, or any form of guided meditation that resonates. Over time, these mindful moments become an integral part of the day, serving as anchors during turbulent times (How to Manage Stress with Mindfulness and Meditation, 2021).

Additionally, integrating mindfulness into existing routines does not require significant lifestyle changes. Instead, it enhances everyday activities with greater presence and awareness. For instance, practicing mindful eating encourages savoring each bite, turning a simple meal into an enriching sensory experience. By fostering gratitude and appreciation for daily occurrences, mindfulness enriches life in meaningful ways.

Integration of Mindfulness for Enhanced Resilience

Incorporating mindfulness into daily practices is a powerful way to foster resilience and manage stress effectively. One of the most transformative practices is regular meditation. By dedicating just a few minutes each day to meditation, individuals can gain greater emotional regulation and awareness, which are crucial foundations for building resilience in stressful situations. Meditation encourages a state of heightened awareness and presence, allowing practitioners to observe their thoughts and emotions without judgment. This practice not only helps in understanding the nature of one's emotional responses but also assists in cultivating a calmer and more balanced mind, serving as a protective barrier against stress (Keng et al., 2011).

Breathing exercises stand out as another vital component in the mindfulness toolkit. By focusing on the breath, either through deep breathing or specific techniques like diaphragmatic breathing, individuals can activate the body's relaxation response. Regular engagement in these exercises enhances long-term emotional resilience by calming the nervous system and reducing stress hormone levels. Over time, this consistent practice increases an individual's capacity to manage stress, making them less reactive and more composed during challenging times (Treatment, 2023).

Mindful walking offers a unique opportunity to integrate mindfulness into everyday routines, providing clarity and uplifting moods naturally. By focusing on each step, feeling the ground beneath your feet, and observing the environment without distraction, you create a state of present-moment awareness. Mindful walking isn't just about movement; it's a full sensory experience that enhances mental clarity and cultivates serenity. The simplicity and accessibility of this practice make it an excellent gateway to mindfulness, especially for those new to the concept (Keng et al., 2011).

Routine body scans deepen the connection between mind and body, further enhancing resilience. This practice involves paying attention to different parts of the body in a systematic manner, noticing sensations without trying to change them. Through regular body scans, individuals become adept at recognizing bodily tension and stress storages, which are often overlooked. By acknowledging these sensations, one can respond with self-care strategies, preventing stress from escalating and promoting a healthier mind-body balance. Practical applications include practicing during bedtime, where it can aid in relaxation and improve sleep quality (Treatment, 2023).

Integrating these practices requires dedication but promises profound benefits. To start, individuals should establish a routine that aligns with their lifestyle. Setting aside specific times for meditation or incorporating short mindful walks into breaks can create consistency. Additionally, using tools like guided meditation apps or joining mindfulness groups can provide structure and community support, enhancing the likelihood of sustained practice (Keng et al., 2011).

For busy professionals, finding time may seem daunting, but even small commitments yield significant results. For instance, starting the day with a brief meditation session can set a positive tone, while lunchtime can be an ideal moment for a quick mindful walk. Evening body scans offer relaxation after a hectic day. Each of these practices, when integrated seamlessly into daily life, builds a robust defense against stress, fostering resilience incrementally.

Ultimately, mindfulness isn't solely about stress management; it's about enriching life through increased awareness and presence. As these practices become embedded in daily routines, individuals often experience enhanced emotional intelligence and empathy, leading to improved relationships both personally and professionally. Such developments contribute to a fuller, more resilient life where stress no longer dominates the landscape of daily experiences.

Wrapping Up

In this chapter, we've explored how mindfulness practices serve as valuable tools for enhancing resilience and managing stress. Through techniques like meditation, deep breathing exercises, mindful walking, and body scans, individuals can cultivate a greater sense of self-awareness and emotional regulation. These practices help anchor us in the present moment, creating a space where we can observe our thoughts and feelings without immediate reaction. This gentle awareness allows us to handle stress more effectively, transforming potential challenges into opportunities for growth and balance. By embracing these mindfulness techniques, we not only quiet the mind but also strengthen our ability to respond to life's ups and downs with clarity and calmness.

As you integrate these mindfulness practices into your daily routine, you'll likely experience an enhanced sense of well-being and resilience. Regular engagement in such exercises nurtures a deeper connection between mind and body, empowering you to recognize and address stress signals proactively. Whether you're navigating the demands of a high-stress profession or seeking personal growth, these simple yet profound practices encourage a life filled with presence and intention. As you continue on this journey, remember that mindfulness is not just about managing stress—it's about enriching every aspect of your life through increased awareness and empathy.

Chapter 12

Narratives of Resilience

R esilience is a defining trait of the human experience, reflecting the remarkable ability of individuals and communities to withstand adversity, adapt to challenges, and emerge stronger. It is not simply about survival but about transformation— turning hardship into growth, setbacks into opportunities, and pain into purpose.

This chapter explores powerful narratives that exemplify resilience in its many forms. From individuals who have overcome personal struggles to communities that have rebuilt after disasters, these stories illustrate the inner strength, adaptability, and support systems that enable people to persevere. Resilience is often forged in the face of adversity—whether it be illness, failure, discrimination, or oppression—and these accounts provide insight into the factors that allow people to endure and thrive.

Through compelling case studies, we will examine resilience across different contexts. Communities coming together in the aftermath of natural disasters demonstrate the power of collective strength, while individuals battling illness highlight the importance of perseverance and self-advocacy. Entrepreneurs who have rebounded from failure showcase the role of adaptability and innovation, while athletes overcoming injuries embody the mental and physical endurance required to push past limitations. These narratives not only celebrate the indomitable human spirit but also offer valuable lessons on determination, collaboration, and the capacity for growth in the face of hardship.

Central to this exploration are the lives of six extraordinary figures—Nelson Mandela, J.K. Rowling, Malala Yousafzai, Steve Jobs, Serena Williams, and Helen Keller—each of whom exemplifies resilience in distinct and profound ways. Their stories reveal that no matter the scale of the challenge—whether it be political imprisonment, rejection, violence, business failure, discrimination, or disability—resilience is the key to overcoming obstacles and leaving a lasting impact on the world.

By understanding their journeys, we gain valuable insights into the nature of persistence, self-belief, and the strategies needed to cultivate resilience in our own lives. Their experiences remind us that setbacks are not the end of the road but rather moments that test our ability to adapt, push forward, and redefine success. Whether facing personal, professional, or societal challenges, these stories serve as powerful testaments to the boundless potential of human resilience.

Principles of Personal Resilience

In facing life's inevitable challenges, resilience emerges as a key trait that can guide individuals through stress and adversity. One of the critical aspects of building resilience is adaptability—the ability to adjust to changing circumstances and recover from setbacks. Adaptability allows individuals to recognize failures not as endpoints but as lessons paving the way for future growth. By examining past experiences and understanding the reasons behind setbacks, people can develop strategies to avoid similar pitfalls in the future. This process of reflection transforms failure from a source of discouragement into a catalyst for personal development (Magic, 2020).

Cultivating a growth mindset is fundamental to embracing change and developing emotional fortitude. A growth mindset encourages the belief that abilities and intelligence can be developed through effort, persistence, and learning. This perspective enables individuals to see challenges as opportunities to grow rather than insurmountable obstacles (Rood, 2023). Embracing a growth mindset fosters resilience by helping individuals remain open to new ideas, approaches, and solutions. It also empowers them to take calculated risks, learn from mistakes, and continuously improve themselves.

Building and maintaining strong social connections is another vital component of resilience. Emotional support from friends, family, and peers provides a safety net during difficult times. These connections offer encouragement, advice, and comfort, which can significantly impact one's ability to cope with stress and adversity. Engaging in community activities, joining support groups, or simply spending quality time with loved ones can boost one's sense of belonging and reduce feelings of isolation (Magic, 2020). Moreover, being part of a supportive network enhances emotional wellbeing and promotes a positive outlook, reinforcing the resilience-building process.

Implementing routines that reinforce resilience-building habits is essential for integrating resilience into daily life. Establishing a consistent routine helps manage stress by providing structure and predictability. Daily practices such as regular exercise, mindful meditation, and journaling can enhance mental and physical well-being, equipping individuals to handle stress more effectively (Rood, 2023). Setting aside time each day for self-care and reflection allows individuals to recharge and gain clarity on their emotions and thoughts. Additionally, incorporating goal-setting into one's routine provides direction and motivation, fostering a proactive approach to overcoming challenges.

A practical guideline for fostering resilience is to start small and gradually build on established habits. Begin by identifying one or two areas where changes could have the most immediate impact. For instance, committing to a 10-minute daily meditation or reaching out to a friend once a week are simple yet effective steps towards building resilience. As these practices become ingrained, they can be expanded and integrated into broader strategies for managing stress and fostering emotional strength. Over time, these incremental changes accumulate, resulting in significant improvements in one's ability to navigate life's ups and downs.

Reflecting on personal experiences can also play a crucial role in developing resilience. Taking the time to assess past reactions to stressors and identifying patterns in behavior can provide valuable insights into how one can better manage future challenges. This reflection encourages self-awareness and highlights areas where growth and adaptation are necessary. By acknowledging vulnerabilities and actively working to address them, individuals empower themselves to face adversity with greater equanimity and resolve (Magic, 2020).

An often overlooked yet powerful element of resilience is the practice of gratitude. Regularly expressing gratitude, whether through journaling or verbal acknowledgment, can shift focus from what is lacking to what is present. This shift in perspective nurtures a more optimistic and resilient mindset, allowing individuals to find joy and strength even amid difficulties. Practicing gratitude can serve as a reminder of the positive aspects of life, enhancing overall well-being and fortifying one's ability to persevere through challenging times.

Case Studies of Resilience

When faced with the wrath of nature, communities often find themselves in situations where resilience is not just an option but a necessity. In the aftermath of natural disasters such as hurricanes or earthquakes, the collective response of a community can serve as a beacon of hope and strength. A notable example is seen when communities band together to clean up debris, rebuild homes, and provide food and shelter to those in need. This collaborative effort emphasizes the power of community support during times of adversity. Community members become anchors for each other, offering both physical help and emotional support. Studies have shown that social networks and collaboration play a critical role in enhancing community resilience, enabling quicker recovery and fostering a sense of unity and shared purpose (Ma et al., 2023).

Individual resilience stories also illuminate the strength of the human spirit. Consider the narrative of someone who has survived a life-threatening illness. Such individuals are often thrust into a world filled with medical jargon, treatments, and hopeful yet uncertain outcomes. Their journey highlights self-advocacy as they navigate the complexities of healthcare, make critical decisions about their treatment, and maintain a positive mindset amidst uncertainty. These survivors demonstrate immense mental fortitude, drawing on inner reserves of strength and the unwavering support of family and friends. Their stories remind us that resilience involves not just bouncing back but growing stronger and wiser from the experience.

In the business world, entrepreneurs playing the comeback game often depict resilience in the face of financial ruin. They confront the challenge of bankruptcy, which can be devastating both financially and emotionally. However, these setbacks are often transformed into opportunities for growth. Entrepreneurs analyze their failures, learn valuable lessons, and apply this newfound knowledge to reposition themselves in the marketplace. The strategy here is clear: viewing failure not as a final defeat but as a stepping stone toward eventual success. This lesson is crucial for professionals across industries, stressing the importance of leveraging failure as part of the growth process (Bakic & Ajdukovic, 2021). Entrepreneurs often reestablish themselves by building networks, seeking mentoring, and adapting their business models to avoid past mistakes. Such strategies highlight the resilience needed to thrive after financial collapse.

Similarly, athletes overcoming significant injuries provide compelling stories of resilience through both mental and physical rehabilitation. Consider an athlete who suffers a debilitating injury, sidetracking their career aspirations. The road to recovery is often long and arduous, requiring dedication, patience, and a strong support system. Physical therapy becomes a daily ritual, pushing the limits of endurance and pain thresholds. Mentally, athletes must battle the fears and doubts that accompany injury, cultivating a mindset focused on recovery and future potential. The psychological aspect of athletic resilience is just as crucial as the physical; embracing the challenge with optimism ensures a return to pre-injury performance levels—or even surpassing them. Guidelines emphasize the importance of setting realistic goals, maintaining motivation, and celebrating small victories along the way. Embracing the power of visualization and self-talk, athletes harness inner determination to overcome setbacks and achieve their goals.

Lessons from Resilient Figures

Nelson Mandela: The Power of Endurance and Forgiveness

Few figures in modern history embody resilience as profoundly as Nelson Mandela. His life is a testament to the idea that resilience is not merely about enduring hardship but about transforming pain into purpose. He demonstrated that true strength lies not in revenge but in reconciliation, and his unwavering commitment to justice and unity reshaped a nation.

Born in 1918 in South Africa, Mandela grew up under the oppressive system of apartheid, a brutal policy of racial segregation that stripped Black South Africans of their basic rights. As a young lawyer, he became actively involved in the anti-apartheid movement, advocating for equality, justice, and the dismantling of institutionalized racism. However, his activism came at a great personal cost.

Imprisonment: The Ultimate Test of Resilience

In 1962, Mandela was arrested for his role in resisting apartheid and was later sentenced to life imprisonment. He spent 27 years behind bars, much of it in harsh conditions on Robben Island, where he was confined to a small cell, subjected to forced labor, and granted only limited contact with the outside world.

For many, such an experience would have led to bitterness, anger, or despair. Yet, Mandela chose a different path. He used his time in prison not to dwell on hatred but to strengthen his mind and spirit. He educated himself, deepened his understanding of leadership, and nurtured a vision for a democratic South Africa. Instead of allowing incarceration to break him, he emerged stronger, wiser, and more determined than ever.

Resilience Through Forgiveness

Mandela's greatest act of resilience came not in his survival but in his response to his suffering. After his release in 1990, rather than seeking retribution against those who had oppressed him, he chose forgiveness. He understood that true resilience is not about holding onto anger but about rising above it.

His leadership was instrumental in guiding South Africa through a peaceful transition from apartheid to democracy. In 1994, he made history by becoming the country's first Black president, a moment that symbolized not only personal triumph but also national healing.

The Legacy of Mandela's Resilience

Mandela's story teaches us that resilience is not just about enduring injustice—it is about responding to adversity with wisdom, patience, and an unwavering commitment to unity. His legacy serves as a powerful reminder that even in the face of overwhelming hardship, forgiveness and reconciliation can be the most profound acts of strength.

The resilience of figures like Nelson Mandela offers invaluable lessons, showing us that challenges—no matter how insurmountable they may seem—can be met with courage, dignity, and a vision for a better future.

J.K. Rowling: Overcoming Rejection and Failure

J.K. Rowling's journey is a powerful testament to persistence, self-belief, and resilience in the face of repeated failure. Before becoming one of the most successful authors of all time with the Harry Potter series, she endured years of personal and professional hardships that tested her determination.

Early Struggles and Setbacks

Rowling's path to success was far from easy. She faced numerous obstacles that could have discouraged her from pursuing her dreams:

- She was a single mother living on government assistance, struggling to make ends meet while raising her daughter.

- She battled depression and financial insecurity, often feeling overwhelmed by the challenges in her life.

- Her Harry Potter manuscript was rejected by 12 different publishers, each of whom dismissed it as commercially unviable.

- She experienced deep personal loss, including the death of her mother, which profoundly influenced her writing and shaped the emotional depth of her stories.

Resilience Through Rejection

Despite these setbacks, Rowling refused to give up on her dream of becoming a published author. She continued to refine her manuscript, improve her storytelling, and persist in submitting her work, convinced that her story had the potential to resonate with readers.

Finally, Bloomsbury Publishing took a chance on Harry Potter and the Philosopher's Stone, setting the stage for one of the greatest literary successes in history. The book became a global phenomenon, selling over 500 million copies worldwide, inspiring an entire generation, and transforming Rowling's life.

Lessons in Resilience

Rowling's story is a powerful reminder that rejection is not the end of the road—it is often part of the journey to success. Rather than allowing failure to discourage her, she used it as motivation to push forward. She later reflected that failure can be a gift because it strips away distractions and forces individuals to focus on what truly matters (Magic, 2020).

Her resilience teaches us that success is often built on a foundation of perseverance, self-belief, and the courage to keep going despite repeated obstacles. Rowling's journey underscores the idea that setbacks are not final— they are stepping stones toward achieving greatness.

Malala Yousafzai: Standing Tall in the Face of Violence

Malala Yousafzai's story is a remarkable testament to courage, determination, and resilience in the face of life-threatening danger. Despite facing violence and oppression, she refused to be silenced, becoming a global advocate for education and human rights.

Targeted for Speaking Out

Born and raised in Pakistan's Swat Valley, Malala grew up in an environment where girls' education was under threat. The Taliban had taken control of the region, imposing strict restrictions that banned girls from attending school.

- From a young age, Malala was deeply passionate about education, believing that every child—regardless of gender—had the right to learn.

- At just 11 years old, she spoke out publicly against these restrictions, writing a blog for the BBC under a pseudonym, detailing the harsh realities of life under the Taliban.

- Her advocacy drew international attention, but it also made her a target.
  In 2012, when Malala was just 15 years old, a Taliban gunman boarded her school bus and shot her in the head, attempting to silence her message forever.

Choosing Resilience Over Fear

Miraculously, Malala survived the attack. Instead of letting fear define her, she chose resilience, refusing to back down from her fight for education.

- Following extensive medical treatment, she continued her activism on an even greater scale, using her near-death experience as a catalyst for change.

- In 2013, she co-authored the memoir I Am Malala, sharing her story with the world and inspiring millions.

- In 2014, at just 17 years old, she became the youngest recipient of the Nobel Peace Prize, cementing her status as a global advocate for education.

Lessons in Resilience

Malala's story is a powerful reminder that resilience is about standing firm in one's beliefs, even in the face of extreme adversity. She transformed violence into activism, fear into courage, and oppression into empowerment.

Her unwavering determination teaches us that one voice— no matter how young—can ignite change. Malala's journey continues to inspire people worldwide, proving that resilience is not just about surviving hardship but about turning adversity into a force for good.

Steve Jobs: Reinventing Failure into Success

Steve Jobs' story is a powerful example of resilience, innovation, and the ability to turn failure into opportunity. Despite experiencing major professional setbacks and personal challenges, he refused to give up on his vision, ultimately revolutionizing the technology industry.

A Visionary Met with Rejection

From an early age, Jobs displayed a passion for technology and innovation. In 1976, he co-founded Apple in his parents' garage, alongside Steve Wozniak, with a vision to make computers accessible to everyday users.

The company quickly grew, introducing groundbreaking products like the Apple II and Macintosh.

- By his late twenties, Jobs was a self-made millionaire, widely recognized as a tech visionary.

- However, success was short-lived—his leadership style clashed with Apple's board, and in 1985, he was forced out of the company he built.

- Facing public humiliation and professional failure, Jobs found himself at a crossroads.

Turning Setbacks into Comebacks

Instead of allowing failure to define him, Jobs chose resilience, using his dismissal from Apple as an opportunity for reinvention.

- He founded NeXT, a company focused on developing high-end computers, which, although not initially successful, later became integral to Apple's future innovations.

- He also purchased Pixar, transforming it into a pioneering animation studio, producing films like Toy Story and redefining the entertainment industry.

- In 1997, Apple—struggling to survive—acquired NeXT, bringing Jobs back to the company he once founded.

Reshaping the Tech Industry

With renewed vision, Jobs led Apple's transformation, introducing game-changing products:

- The iMac, which revived Apple's brand and set new standards in design.
- The iPod and iTunes, which revolutionized digital music.
- The iPhone and iPad, which changed how people interact with technology worldwide.

His ability to turn failure into a stepping stone for success cemented his legacy as one of the greatest innovators of all time.

Serena Williams: Dominating Against All Odds

Serena Williams' journey is a powerful example of resilience, perseverance, and the determination to overcome obstacles. Despite facing discrimination, injuries, and intense scrutiny throughout her career, she refused to let adversity define her, ultimately becoming one of the greatest athletes of all time.

Breaking Barriers in a Tough Sport

From an early age, Williams displayed an unwavering passion for tennis, training alongside her sister Venus under the guidance of their father, Richard Williams. However, as young Black athletes in a predominantly white and elitist sport, they faced numerous challenges:

- Critics doubted their potential, questioning whether they belonged in the world of professional tennis.

- Serena faced racism and sexism, both on and off the court, as she challenged the norms of a traditionally exclusive sport.

- She endured financial struggles early in her career, training on public courts rather than at elite tennis academies.

Despite these barriers, she remained laser-focused on her goals, determined to prove her worth through sheer talent and relentless effort.

Overcoming Setbacks and Injuries

As Serena climbed to the top, she encountered significant setbacks, including:

- Severe injuries, including knee and foot problems, that threatened to derail her career.

- Life-threatening health complications, such as pulmonary embolisms following the birth of her daughter.

- Criticism and controversy, often targeted at her body, style of play, and competitive spirit.

Many athletes would have succumbed to these challenges, but Serena chose resilience, returning stronger each time. Her ability to adapt, push through pain, and maintain mental toughness set her apart from her peers.

Redefining Greatness in Sports

Williams' relentless drive led to a career filled with unparalleled achievements:

- 23 Grand Slam singles titles, the most by any player in the Open Era.

- 319 weeks as world No. 1, proving her dominance across generations.

- Four Olympic gold medals, highlighting her versatility and longevity.

Beyond her titles, Serena transformed the sport, becoming a role model for young athletes, especially women and people of color, inspiring them to break barriers and chase their dreams .

Lessons in Resilience

Serena Williams' journey is a testament to the power of determination, hard work, and self-belief. She faced countless obstacles—yet never let them define her.

Her story teaches us that true resilience is about rising after every fall, facing adversity head-on, and pushing beyond perceived limits. Williams continues to inspire millions, proving that greatness is not just about talent—it's about the relentless will to succeed despite the odds.

Helen Keller: Triumph Over Physical Adversity

Helen Keller's story is one of the most extraordinary examples of resilience, determination, and the power of perseverance. Despite being deaf and blind from infancy, she defied expectations, proving that physical limitations do not define a person's potential. With the right mindset, support, and determination, she transformed obstacles into opportunities and became a renowned author, activist, and advocate for disability rights.

Overcoming the Impossible

Born in 1880 in Tuscumbia, Alabama, Keller lost her sight and hearing at just 19 months old due to an illness, leaving her trapped in a world of silence and darkness.

- As a child, she struggled with communication and frustration, unable to express her thoughts or understand those around her.

- Many believed she would never be able to learn, communicate, or live independently.

- However, her life changed at age seven, when she met Anne Sullivan, the teacher who would unlock her potential.

Finding a Voice Through Perseverance

With Sullivan's guidance, Keller embarked on an extraordinary journey of learning and self-discovery.

- She learned to communicate through touch and sign language, gradually mastering Braille, reading, writing, and even speech.

- Her determination to learn led her to Radcliffe College, where she became the first deafblind person to earn a college degree.

- She refused to be limited by her disabilities, proving that intellect and ambition are not bound by physical constraints.

A Champion for Disability Rights

Instead of allowing her struggles to define or confine her, Keller used her experiences to advocate for others.

- She became a leading voice for people with disabilities, fighting for education, accessibility, and equal opportunities.

- She traveled the world as a lecturer and activist, inspiring millions with her story.

- Her work with organizations like the American Foundation for the Blind transformed public perception of disability.

Lessons in Resilience

Helen Keller's life is a testament to the power of determination, adaptability, and support. Her journey teaches us that resilience is not about avoiding obstacles but about learning how to overcome them.

Her story reminds us that limitations only exist if we accept them. Through perseverance, education, and the right support system, anyone can rise above challenges and turn adversity into a source of strength.

Final Thoughts

Throughout this chapter, we have explored powerful stories of resilience, demonstrating how individuals and communities rise to challenges with unwavering strength. From communities rebuilding after natural disasters to individuals overcoming illness, failure, and discrimination, a common thread emerges: the power of perseverance and adaptability. These stories remind us that resilience is not reserved for extraordinary circumstances or exceptional individuals—it is an inherent quality that everyone can cultivate.

Resilience is about more than just enduring hardship; it is about growing from setbacks and using those experiences as stepping stones to a stronger future. The narratives of Nelson Mandela and Malala Yousafzai further illustrate that resilience is not only a personal trait but a force for societal change. Their ability to transform adversity into movements for justice, equality, and empowerment demonstrates the profound impact that staying committed to one's values can have on the world.

As we reflect on these stories, it becomes clear that resilience is built through adaptability, strong support systems, and a growth mindset. Whether facing personal struggles, professional setbacks, or societal challenges, these principles serve as a guide for fostering resilience in our own lives.

The journeys of Nelson Mandela, J.K. Rowling, Malala Yousafzai, Steve Jobs, Serena Williams, and Helen Keller highlight the universal nature of resilience—spanning literature, business, sports, activism, and beyond. Their experiences reinforce key lessons:

- Failure is not final—it often serves as a stepping stone to success.

- Adaptability and perseverance are crucial in overcoming obstacles.

- Support systems and community play a vital role in resilience.

By embracing these principles, we can navigate life's challenges with confidence and determination, understanding that every setback is an opportunity for future growth. Resilience is not just about surviving—it is about thriving, learning, and pushing forward with optimism and purpose.

Chapter 13

The Support System

Having a solid support system can greatly enhance one's ability to cope with stress and adversity. With so much going on in life, it's easy to feel overwhelmed, yet the right kind of social support can make all the difference. In this chapter, we explore the power of social connections and how they contribute to building resilience. The role of family, friends, and even broader community ties is more significant than one might initially assume. Not only do these relationships provide comfort, but they also foster an environment that encourages growth, adaptability, and strength during difficult times. By tapping into the potential of our social networks, we unlock new ways to rise above life's challenges.

We delve into strategies for identifying, maintaining, and expanding your network of support. From recognizing those who truly stand by you to engaging with community resources, this chapter outlines practical steps to fortify personal and professional connections. Readers will discover how nurturing these relationships enhances emotional well-being and provides a buffer against stressors. Furthermore, the chapter highlights various ways to utilize modern tools like social media to strengthen these bonds, offering guidance on balancing digital interactions with real-world connections. Through these insights, individuals are equipped with the knowledge to turn their social environments into powerful sources of resilience, ensuring they are never alone in facing life's hurdles.

Building a Supportive Network

Building a robust support network is essential for bolstering resilience, especially in times of stress and adversity. This subpoint focuses on creating and nurturing relationships that offer genuine support, thereby enhancing one's capacity to bounce back from life's challenges.

To begin with, identifying those who provide authentic support in your life is a critical step in fortifying resilience. These individuals are the ones you turn to in moments of difficulty, who listen without judgment, offer wise counsel, and encourage you through tough times. They could be family members, friends, colleagues, or mentors—anyone who stands by you when the going gets tough. Recognizing these key players in your life not only strengthens your personal sense of security but also cultivates an environment where resilience can thrive. Understanding who genuinely supports you allows you to focus your energy and emotional investments wisely, ensuring that you have reliable allies during challenging times (Suttie, 2017).

Expanding your social circle is another crucial aspect of building resilience. Engaging in community activities provides opportunities to meet like-minded individuals who could become valuable additions to your support network. Whether it's joining a local sports team, attending workshops, volunteering, or participating in social clubs, these interactions foster connections that bring fresh perspectives and shared experiences. Community engagement helps build a sense of belonging and can introduce you to people who share similar interests or goals, further broadening your social support map. When you surround yourself with diverse individuals who nourish your well-being, you create a buffer against life's adversities.

Maintaining existing relationships requires consistent communication to keep them strong and supportive. Regular check-ins, whether through phone calls, text messages, video chats, or face-to-face meetings, help keep the connection alive. Even small gestures, such as sending thoughtful messages or remembering significant dates, show appreciation and care, reinforcing these bonds. Over time, regular interaction builds trust and understanding, making it easier to reach out for support when needed. Moreover, being proactive in your engagements ensures that your relationships remain balanced and mutually beneficial, thus contributing positively to your emotional health (Social Connection Builds Resilience, 2020).

In today's digital age, social media platforms serve as powerful tools for enhancing connections. They provide a space where maintaining relationships is more flexible, allowing for communication across distances and busy schedules. Online interactions can supplement face-to-face communication, offering additional ways to stay connected with those who matter. Social media can be particularly useful in keeping in touch with friends and family who live far away, enabling frequent updates and interactions that help maintain closeness.

While some may argue that online interactions lack the depth of in-person connections, they still play a vital role in keeping relationships vibrant. A simple comment on a friend's post or a shared article can spark conversations and keep the relationship dynamic. Moreover, social media opens doors to new communities and support groups, where individuals can connect over shared interests or experiences. Such communities can provide a sense of belonging and access to advice, resources, and encouragement from peers who understand your journey.

However, it's important to approach social media mindfully, recognizing its potential pitfalls. Use it to enhance real-world connections and avoid substituting face-to-face interactions entirely. Striking a balance between online and offline communication ensures that your social networks contribute positively to your resilience rather than detract from it.

Leaning on Family and Friends

In times of adversity, the support of close family and friends serves as a crucial cornerstone in fostering resilience. Recognizing who among them is emotionally available can significantly diminish feelings of isolation. When challenges arise, having someone who listens and empathizes provides a sense of belonging and understanding, mitigating loneliness and enhancing one's ability to cope. Emotional availability is not just being physically present; it implies an engagement that conveys empathy and allows vulnerability.

To truly benefit from such a support system, it's essential to communicate needs clearly. This openness not only clarifies expectations but also deepens familial connections. For instance, expressing emotions or seeking advice can make interactions more meaningful. When family members understand each other's needs, it fortifies relationships, creating a robust network capable of withstanding life's trials. Open communication transforms these connections into pillars of strength, reinforcing the idea that one is never alone in their struggles.

Facing challenges together with loved ones offers a unique opportunity to build resilience mutually. When families unite during difficult moments, they share experiences that teach perseverance and adaptability. The collective effort of tackling problems reinforces shared values and trust, laying the groundwork for enduring partnerships. Consider how families might come together to support a member undergoing therapy or recovering from a setback. Such shared experiences can cultivate resilience, not only for the individual directly affected but for everyone involved, highlighting the power of unity in overcoming obstacles.

Family and friends also play a pivotal role in providing encouragement and accountability. Their constant presence and genuine care act as a motivational force, propelling individuals towards personal growth. For example, when embarking on a new goal, having a supportive circle can offer the necessary nudges to stay committed. Friends and family remind us of our capabilities and celebrate even small victories, which nurtures confidence and motivation. They hold us accountable, ensuring that we remain focused and dedicated to our pursuits, thereby fostering a culture of continuous improvement and learning.

The influence of these relationships extends beyond emotional support, contributing significantly to mental health and well-being. Research underscores the importance of incorporating close ties in cognitive behavioral therapy (CBT) programs, revealing that individuals with supportive family members achieve better progress than those without such backing. Family involvement in mental health journeys reinforces the therapeutic process, emphasizing the positive outcomes of having a steadfast support system (Learn, 2023). This connection between social support and mental health stresses the necessity of nurturing strong family bonds.

Social support's impact is complex, shaped by both the nature of the support and the needs of those receiving it. While the size of one's social network matters, it's the perception of beneficial interactions that truly counts. Feeling cared for and respected by others instills comfort, promoting a strong foundation for resilience. Understanding this dynamic highlights the multifaceted nature of social support and its diverse manifestations across different systems, such as family or community networks, which are instrumental in shaping resilience (Southwick et al., 2016).

Leveraging Social Media

In an age where personal and professional lives often intersect with digital spheres, harnessing technology to enhance social connections has become essential. Online communities provide vital support for those who may find themselves isolated due to geographical barriers or personal circumstances. These virtual spaces are not just substitutes for face-to-face interactions but offer unique opportunities that can significantly contribute to one's resilience.

Online communities cater to a wide array of interests, from health and wellness groups to fandom forums and professional networks. For individuals experiencing isolation, these communities can mimic traditional support systems, offering companionship and understanding in challenging times. According to research, the sense of belonging fostered within online spaces can alleviate loneliness and even improve mental health outcomes by creating environments where members feel valued and understood (Oksanen et al., 2024).

Digital communication tools further enhance these connections by offering remarkable flexibility in how relationships are maintained. Unlike traditional methods that require physical presence or synchronous meeting, platforms like video calls, messaging apps, and emails allow people to communicate at their own pace, on their own schedules. This flexibility is particularly beneficial for professionals in high-stress jobs, enabling them to reach out to others for support without the pressure of coordinating busy calendars.

Moreover, digital platforms serve as a conduit for support groups that operate beyond geographical limitations. Various websites and applications provide safe spaces for individuals to share experiences, receive advice, and find solace in shared struggles. These platforms amplify the voices of diverse groups, empowering members to connect over common narratives, which can be especially valuable for those dealing with specific issues such as chronic illnesses or mental health challenges (Can Social Media and Online Communities Be Good for Us? | Psychology Today, n.d.).

There is also a significant opportunity to use social media to build and expand one's network. By utilizing social media wisely, individuals can tap into broader communities that extend beyond immediate circles, opening doors for personal and professional growth. Professional sites like LinkedIn facilitate networking with industry peers, while interest-based groups on platforms like Facebook can strengthen both personal connections and subject matter expertise.

Navigating these digital spaces requires a mindful approach to ensure that the benefits outweigh potential drawbacks. While engaging in virtual communities, it is crucial to maintain a balance between digital interactions and real-world experiences. Demonstrating appreciation for supportive individuals, whether online or offline, helps nurture reciprocal relationships and reinforces these connections as durable elements of one's social network.

The power of technology in enhancing connections lies not only in overcoming physical barriers but also in cultivating the kind of emotional support that sustains resilience. For instance, during times of crisis, having established online relationships can provide a solid safety net. Knowing that help is just a message away can bring comfort and reduce feelings of vulnerability.

Final Insights

Understanding the power of social connections is vital in building resilience. Throughout this chapter, we explored how fostering meaningful relationships can provide immense support during challenging times. By identifying those who offer genuine support and expanding your social network through community engagement, you weave a safety net that bolsters emotional strength. Maintaining these connections requires regular communication, which strengthens trust and creates a reliable support system. In addition, leveraging digital tools and social media enables maintaining and expanding relationships across distances, enhancing your circle of support. Balancing online interactions with in-person experiences enriches these bonds, offering a well-rounded approach to resilience.

In the face of adversity, family and friends offer a foundation of comfort and encouragement, helping diminish feelings of isolation. Through clear communication of needs, these relationships deepen, transforming into pillars of mutual strength. Facing challenges together builds collective resilience, as shared experiences foster perseverance and adaptability.

Accessing digital communities further broadens the opportunity for connection and growth, providing a sense of belonging and understanding. As this chapter highlights, nurturing diverse social networks not only enhances individual well-being but also forms an essential part of a resilient life. Embrace these connections and let them fortify your journey toward greater resilience and personal growth.

Chapter 14

The Resilient Leader

L eadership with resilience stands as a necessary skill in navigating today's ever-changing and challenging environments. It involves more than just strategic planning or decision-making; it demands an intrinsic understanding of interpersonal dynamics and individual strengths. This kind of leadership is not about avoiding difficulties but confronting them head-on, equipped with empathy, adaptability, and vision. The resilient leader thrives by cultivating a mindset open to growth, continuously learning from experiences, whether successes or setbacks. By recognizing the unique challenges that come with leading under pressure, these leaders not only endure trials but also emerge stronger, guiding their teams toward shared goals with determination and optimism.

In this chapter, we delve into the distinctive traits that define resilient leaders, examining how self-awareness, empathy, adaptability, and vision contribute to their effectiveness. Through descriptive exploration, you'll discover practical approaches for fostering these attributes within yourself and your team. Learn how self-awareness enables leaders to balance personal growth with collaborative efforts and how practicing empathy enhances team cohesion. Explore the significance of maintaining a clear vision during tumultuous times and understand the necessity of adaptability in response to change. The insights offered aim to equip you with tools and perspectives that bolster your leadership capabilities, ultimately empowering both your personal and professional journey amidst adversity.

Traits of Resilient Leaders

Exploring the essential traits of resilient leaders unveils a blueprint for navigating adversity and inspiring teams. Central to this discussion is self-awareness, a fundamental trait that involves an introspective understanding of one's own strengths and weaknesses. By acknowledging their limitations, leaders can effectively identify areas where support is needed, embrace collaboration, and pursue personal growth strategies. This self-reflective practice not only enhances their decision-making capabilities but also fosters a culture of openness within their teams, encouraging members to recognize their own potential and areas for improvement.

A practical step towards cultivating self-awareness is setting aside time for regular reflection. Leaders can maintain journals detailing instances where they excelled as well as scenarios requiring assistance or adjustment.

Engaging in feedback sessions with colleagues or mentors further broadens insight into their leadership style, facilitating the refinement of strategic approaches.

Empathy forms another cornerstone of resilient leadership. This ability to connect emotionally with team members is crucial for building an inclusive environment where everyone feels valued and heard. Empathetic leaders demonstrate genuine concern for the well-being and perspectives of others, thereby fostering trustful relationships and enhancing team cohesion. Such environments are vital during challenging periods, as they provide employees with a secure space to voice concerns and suggestions without fear of retribution.

Leaders looking to enhance empathy should practice active listening by giving undivided attention during conversations, withholding judgment, and responding thoughtfully. Encouraging regular check-ins or informal discussions provides opportunities to better understand team dynamics and individual challenges.

Vision, while not requiring specific guidelines, acts as a beacon, providing clear direction and purpose not just in smooth sailing, but more critically in turbulent times. It empowers leaders to guide their teams through uncertainty, inspiring hope and motivation. A well-communicated vision aligns individuals towards shared goals, reinforcing their commitment despite facing obstacles. Leaders who articulate a compelling vision motivate their teams to look beyond present difficulties and focus on long-term success.

To maintain a strong vision, leaders should communicate it frequently and adapt it when necessary to accommodate changing circumstances. Regularly sharing stories that epitomize the organization's values and aspirations helps reinforce its importance and resonate with team members on a personal level.

Adaptability stands as a pivotal trait for resilient leaders, enabling them to adjust strategies and processes dynamically in response to evolving circumstances. Rapid changes in the business landscape demand innovative and creative problem-solving skills, which adaptable leaders are well-equipped to offer. By embracing change rather than resisting it, these leaders model a flexible mindset for their teams, encouraging them to experiment with new ideas and approaches.

Effective adaptability requires a willingness to learn from past experiences and apply those lessons to current situations. Leaders can facilitate adaptability by fostering a workspace open to experimentation, where mistakes are viewed as learning opportunities rather than failures. Encouraging cross-functional collaboration allows teams to draw insights from diverse fields, spurring innovative solutions to complex problems.

Resilience in Team Building

In today's fast-paced world, where challenges and uncertainties seem to lurk around every corner, fostering resilience within teams becomes a cornerstone for success. Resilient teams are not just groups of individuals working together; they are cohesive units capable of overcoming obstacles with grace and determination. At the heart of this approach is the steadfast belief that resilience can be nurtured through a blend of supportive culture, clear communication, defined expectations, and continuous growth opportunities.

Creating a supportive culture is essential in laying the foundation for team resilience. Such a culture thrives on collaboration and mutual support, encouraging team members to lean on one another during challenging times. Celebrate small wins as they occur; this practice not only boosts morale but also serves as a constant reminder of progress, no matter how incremental. Leaders play a crucial role here, as their behavior sets the tone for the entire group. By modeling supportive behavior themselves —listening actively, prioritizing empathy, and reinforcing positive interactions—they invite team members to follow suit. This environment diminishes stress levels and enhances overall well-being, making it easier for everyone to face challenges with a united front. As Maven (n.d.)

outlines, strong communication skills are integral to fostering these relationships.

Open communication acts as a vital conduit for transparency and problem-solving within resilient teams. Encouraging team members to voice their concerns without fear of reprisal cultivates an atmosphere of trust and openness. Regularly scheduled meetings provide a platform for team members to share updates, offer insights, and collaborate on solutions, thus reducing ambiguity and ensuring everyone remains aligned. This transparency becomes particularly valuable when the team encounters unexpected challenges, as members are already accustomed to open dialogue. In fact, it's not just about having conversations but fostering a culture where feedback is welcomed. When leaders show that they value input from all levels, team members feel empowered to contribute their unique perspectives, enhancing the team's ability to adapt and innovate in real-time. Good (2024) emphasizes the importance of transparent communication as a trust-building tactic.

Setting clear expectations is another critical aspect of building resilient teams. When roles and responsibilities are clearly defined, team members have a better understanding of what is expected of them, which reduces confusion and potential conflict. This clarity allows individuals to focus on their tasks and collaborate more effectively with others, knowing exactly where their contributions fit into the larger picture. Clear expectations also aid in holding everyone accountable, as there is a mutual understanding of goals and standards. When team members know what is required of them, they become more adaptable to changes because they have a firm grasp of their core duties and how they might evolve. Furthermore, setting realistic and achievable targets prevents burnout and keeps the team motivated to strive towards collective accomplishments. Celebrating these accomplishments, as proposed by Good (2024), reinforces the sense of achievement and motivation.

Opportunities for personal and professional growth serve as powerful motivators within resilient teams. Providing pathways for development not only enhances individual skill sets but also boosts team morale and loyalty. When team members see that their organization values continuous learning and recognizes the potential within each individual, they feel more engaged and committed to their work. Offering workshops, mentorship programs, or access to online courses can equip team members with new skills, making them more confident and versatile when facing industry challenges. Continuous learning fosters a mindset that embraces change and views challenges as opportunities rather than setbacks. Organizations like Amazon exemplify this by offering programs that assist employees in acquiring skills beyond their current roles, creating an adaptable workforce ready for future demands. Maven (n.d.) notes the value of skill development in strengthening a team's adaptability.

Strategies for Leading Resilient Teams

Leading with resilience in challenging environments requires adaptive strategies that go beyond the conventional playbook. One pivotal strategy involves implementing flexible leadership approaches to address the diverse needs of team members while maintaining overall cohesion. In a fast-paced world, teams often face varying demands, requiring leaders to adjust their style and methods accordingly. Consider a leader managing a global team; they must navigate cultural differences and time zones by offering flexible work hours and adopting agile communication tools, reflecting an adaptable approach to maintain unity while respecting individual dynamics (CDP, 2024).

Moreover, promoting a learning environment is integral for continuous improvement and adaptability. In environments where change is constant, resilience is bolstered when team members are encouraged to learn continuously and refine their skills. Imagine a tech company facing rapid innovation cycles. Here, leaders can organize regular training sessions and workshops, fostering a culture where acquiring new knowledge becomes second nature. This not only equips employees for evolving scenarios but also cultivates a mindset where challenges are viewed as opportunities for growth, reinforcing the team's adaptive capabilities (CDP, 2024).

Leveraging tough experiences as learning points is another crucial strategy for building collective team resilience. Every setback or challenge experienced by a team holds valuable lessons that, when harnessed effectively, strengthen the group's problem-solving abilities. Encouraging reflective practices, such as post-project reviews or debriefs, allows teams to analyze what went wrong, what could be improved, and how successes were achieved. For instance, after completing a challenging project, a managed reflection session can help the team identify key takeaways that inform future endeavors. Such practices ensure that past difficulties translate into practical wisdom, fortifying the team for future challenges.

Regular feedback sessions play a vital role in contributing to robust team dynamics by addressing potential issues proactively. Open lines of communication ensure that concerns are aired before they escalate into significant problems, fostering a trusting environment where team members feel heard and valued. Leaders who prioritize regular one-on-one meetings and team feedback gatherings create a culture of transparency and collaboration. Consider a healthcare leader regularly meeting with nurses to discuss workflow challenges and patient care improvements. This proactive engagement not only resolves minor issues swiftly but also empowers the team with a sense of agency, enhancing morale and performance (Farrell, 2024).

Incorporating these strategies requires a thoughtful approach to leadership where adaptability and foresight are central. Leaders must remain vigilant about the changing landscape and its implications on team dynamics. By embodying flexibility themselves, they model the behavior expected from their teams, encouraging open-mindedness and innovation. Furthermore, investing in leadership development programs can equip leaders with the necessary skills to mentor teams through uncertainties, ensuring a supportive and inclusive environment conducive to resilience (Farrell, 2024).

Another important aspect of leading resilient teams is the establishment of clear goals and direction. Team members should understand the organization's objectives and how their roles contribute to this bigger picture. Without clarity, teams may struggle with alignment, leading to inefficiencies and frustration. Therefore, leaders should consistently communicate the mission and vision, breaking down complex goals into manageable tasks that provide a roadmap for success. Through regular reviews and adjustments, a clear path is maintained even amidst changing circumstances, empowering the team to stay focused and motivated.

Additionally, investing in continuous learning and development fosters a culture of perpetual growth. As industries evolve, so too should the skill sets within your team. Providing resources and opportunities for professional development not only enhances individual capabilities but also prepares the team collectively to tackle unforeseen challenges. Companies can achieve this by offering access to online courses, hosting industry experts for seminars, or facilitating peer learning sessions where team members share insights from their areas of expertise (CDP, 2024).

Bringing It All Together

In the unfolding journey through this chapter, we have delved into the vital traits that define resilient leadership. By focusing on self-awareness, leaders are better equipped to navigate both personal and professional challenges with confidence. Recognizing one's strengths and areas for growth allows for a more collaborative and supportive environment within teams, setting the stage for open communication and mutual respect. Meanwhile, empathy stands as an important pillar in building connections, ensuring that team members feel understood and valued. This fosters trust and unity, especially when navigating difficult times together. The guiding force of a clear vision empowers leaders to inspire their teams towards shared objectives, even amidst uncertainty. In embracing adaptability, leaders reveal how shifting perspectives can lead to innovative solutions that propel teams forward.

Building resilience within teams extends beyond merely enduring challenges; it's about thriving amid them and using them as stepping stones toward success. By cultivating a supportive culture where individuals lean on each other, celebrating even small victories, team cohesion is strengthened. Enabling open dialogue without fear encourages transparent communication, aligning everyone with shared goals despite unforeseen hurdles. Clear expectations eliminate confusion and foster accountability, creating a foundation where adaptability to change is not only possible but embraced. Providing opportunities for growth fuels motivation and equips individuals with versatile skills to tackle industry demands. Through these strategies, the blueprint for leading with resilience emerges, offering practical insights for navigating the complex landscapes of personal and professional life.

Chapter 15

Practical Exercises for Building Resilience

B uilding resilience through practical exercises is a transformative journey that empowers individuals to face life's challenges with greater strength and mental fortitude. In today's fast-paced world, where stress and adversity are ever-present, developing resilience has become more crucial than ever. This chapter introduces a variety of actionable strategies that not only enhance emotional intelligence but also foster personal growth. By embedding these practices into daily routines, readers can build the resilience needed to navigate both personal and professional landscapes with confidence and composure.

Within this chapter, you will discover an array of exercises designed to strengthen resilience comprehensively. You'll start with a morning mindset routine aimed at setting a positive tone for the day, enhancing clarity, motivation, and productivity. As the day progresses, midday self-assessments provide opportunities for introspection and emotional growth, equipping you with tools to manage stress effectively. Visualization and affirmation techniques further cultivate a resilient mindset, enabling you to envision success and reinforce self-belief. Additionally, evening journaling serves as a reflective practice to process experiences and set intentions, rounding off your resilience-building efforts. Each exercise integrates seamlessly into daily life, promising profound improvements in well-being and mental strength over time.

Daily Resilience Workout

The pursuit of resilience is an ongoing journey, one that can be enriched by integrating specific practices into our daily lives. A powerful way to begin this journey is by establishing a morning mindset routine. This routine involves setting aside time each morning to focus on activities that enhance your mental clarity and motivation for the day ahead. The goal here is to cultivate a habit that not only builds resilience but also boosts your productivity and overall well-being.

A practical guideline for forming a morning mindset ritual involves several steps. Start with simple actions like stretching or a brief meditation session designed to center your thoughts and clear away any lingering stress from the previous day. This quiet moment allows you to transition smoothly into a focused state. Incorporating gratitude exercises, such as listing three things you are thankful for, can significantly elevate your mood and set a positive tone for the day. According to research, practicing gratitude reduces stress levels and enhances emotional resilience (Ryan Zofay Author Coach & Speaker, 2024).

Midday provides an opportunity to check in with yourself through self-assessments. These assessments are vital in building emotional intelligence and developing problem-solving skills. Take a few minutes to evaluate how you are feeling emotionally and mentally. Are there tasks or interactions that have impacted your mood? Reflect on these experiences and identify patterns that may arise. This practice encourages a deeper understanding of your reactions and empowers you to adapt more effectively to challenges. For instance, recognizing how a stressful meeting affects you can help you prepare better for future situations, fostering adaptability and resilience.

An effective technique during these midday self-assessments is to ask yourself reflective questions. Consider prompts like "What feelings am I experiencing right now, and why?" or "What strengths have I demonstrated today?" These questions not only promote introspection but also help reinforce a sense of self-awareness and control, crucial aspects of emotional intelligence. By regularly engaging with these reflections, individuals can build a toolkit of strategies to manage adversity more effectively, strengthening their personal resilience over time (100 Journal Prompts for Self-Growth with Examples - Brahmas Natural Incense, 2023).

Another cornerstone of resilience-building is utilizing affirmation and visualization techniques. Positive affirmations are statements that reinforce optimistic beliefs about oneself. Spend a few minutes each day repeating affirmations that resonate with you, such as "I am capable of overcoming any obstacle" or "I am continuously growing". This practice helps reshape negative thought patterns into positive ones, laying the foundation for a resilient mindset. As research suggests, affirmations boost confidence and promote a more positive self-image (Ryan Zofay Author Coach & Speaker, 2024).

Visualization complements affirmations by encouraging you to envisage success and resilience. Picture yourself handling difficult situations with calmness and poise. Imagine achieving your goals and the steps you took to get there. This mental rehearsal strengthens your belief in your capabilities and prepares you to face real-world challenges with greater assurance. Studies show that such visualization practices not only enhance motivation but also improve actual performance by aligning your mental state with your desired outcomes.

Evening reflection through journaling offers a meaningful way to close the day, providing space to process emotions and set intentions for the future. Writing down your thoughts, feelings, and reflections on the day's events can illuminate insights into your behavior and decision-making processes. This act of self-expression allows you to release pent-up emotions, making room for clearer thinking and improved mental health.

When journaling in the evening, consider writing about moments of resilience you displayed and areas where you felt challenged. Exploring questions like "What did I learn from today's experiences?" or "How can I apply these lessons moving forward?" can deepen your understanding of personal growth. Additionally, setting goals or intentions for the next day can inspire a sense of direction and purpose. Journaling becomes not only a tool for reflection but also a vehicle for envisioning a resilient future.

Resilience Journaling

Journaling stands as a powerful tool for enhancing resilience, offering individuals the means to navigate life's challenges with greater clarity and strength. At its core, creating a dedicated resilience journal allows readers to track personal growth and confront challenges head-on. This practice involves setting aside time to document experiences, emotions, and reflections regularly. By doing so, individuals build a narrative of their resilience journey, facilitating deeper self-awareness and personal transformation over time.

To embark on this journey, one needs only a simple notebook or digital device—whichever medium feels most comfortable. The key is to create a habit, an oasis in the midst of daily life, where one can reflect without judgment. As noted by WebMD (2021), journaling provides essential separation from consuming thoughts, allowing individuals to process stress and cultivate emotional healing. In this safe space, the act of writing down experiences helps unpack complex feelings and situations, enabling a more objective view that leads to constructive outcomes.

A particularly effective method within journaling is the use of prompted techniques. Prompts serve as catalysts for introspection, encouraging users to delve into specific themes or emotions. This structure not only aids in overcoming writer's block but also ensures that each entry serves a meaningful purpose. For instance, prompts might include questions like "What challenge did I overcome today?" or "What am I grateful for despite current struggles?" Such exercises nurture optimism by directing focus away from obstacles toward achievements and positive aspects of life. Fredrickson (2010) highlighted that focusing on gratitude through journaling can amplify positivity, leading to improved mental well-being.

Over time, the practice of journaling unveils patterns of growth and resilience strategies. Revisiting past entries allows individuals to recognize recurring themes or triggers, mapping out their emotional landscape. This ongoing analysis is crucial for developing coping mechanisms tailored to one's unique experiences. Sutton (2018) emphasized that being mindful of these patterns fosters acceptance of emotions, a cornerstone for psychological health. Journaling thus becomes a vital tool in understanding and adapting to new challenges with greater ease.

Sharing insights gleaned from journaling can further enrich the resilience-building process. Discussing journal reflections with peers offers an opportunity to gain diverse perspectives, fostering a sense of community and support. These conversations can introduce new ways of thinking about resilience, highlighting the commonality of struggles and the potential for shared solutions. According to Tartakovsky (2022), social support contributes significantly to emotional recovery and resilience, making it an invaluable component of the journaling journey.

To integrate journaling effectively into one's routine, consistency is key. Setting aside even a few minutes daily can transform this practice into a foundational element of resilience development. Koschalk (2023) suggests starting small, perhaps with just five minutes a day, before gradually extending the duration as comfort with the process grows. This gentle approach minimizes initial resistance and helps establish journaling as a soothing, reflective habit.

Additionally, experimenting with various types of journaling can cater to different needs and preferences. Some may find solace in expressive writing, which focuses on raw emotional expression without concern for form or grammar. Others might gravitate towards gratitude journals, emphasizing positive reflections and encouraging a mindset shift towards appreciation. The diversity of journaling styles ensures that everyone can find a method that resonates deeply, supporting their unique resilience journey.

While the practice of journaling can sometimes evoke difficult emotions, the long-term benefits outweigh the immediate discomfort. Writing permits the airing of frustrations in a safe, non-judgmental environment, offering clarity and perspective. As Newman (2020) observed, the temporary distress felt during writing often leads to enhanced mental wellbeing and emotional regulation over time. This cathartic process assists in reducing anxiety and obsessive thought cycles, promoting overall psychological balance.

Furthermore, tracking progress through journaling equips individuals with tangible evidence of personal development. Reviewing entries provides motivation by showcasing past victories and illustrating one's capacity to overcome adversity. This ongoing documentation bolsters self-esteem and confidence, reinforcing belief in one's ability to handle future challenges with resilience and grace. The iterative nature of journaling thus creates a feedback loop of empowerment and growth.

Visualization and Affirmation Techniques

In the journey of building resilience, visualization emerges as a powerful technique that can significantly influence mental fortitude. Visualization involves creating detailed mental images of desired outcomes and success in various situations. By regularly practicing visualization, individuals can cultivate a mindset that is not only prepared to face challenges but also thrives amidst them.

Imagine gearing up for an important presentation at work. By visualizing yourself delivering the presentation confidently, engaging the audience, and responding adeptly to questions, you set the stage for success. This mental rehearsal not only reduces anxiety but also enhances self-belief, equipping you with the confidence needed to handle high-pressure scenarios. Athletes have long embraced this practice, visualizing themselves achieving their goals, which ultimately prepares both mind and body for actual performance.

Visualization works by engaging multiple senses, making it a profound exercise in mental training. For instance, when envisioning a serene beach, consider the warmth of the sun, the gentle sound of waves, and the fresh scent of ocean air. This sensory engagement creates a rich, immersive experience that strengthens neural pathways associated with positivity and resilience.

Positive affirmations complement visualization by transforming negative thought patterns into constructive ones. Affirmations are short, uplifting statements repeated consistently to influence one's mindset positively. They act as antidotes to self-doubt, gradually replacing ingrained negativity with empowering beliefs.

To incorporate affirmations effectively, personalizing them is key. Tailor affirmations to your specific goals or challenges. For example, if you struggle with self-doubt during stressful situations, an affirmation like "I am calm, capable, and confident" can be beneficial. By anchoring these affirmations with visualizations, the connection between belief and behavior is fortified, encouraging a resilient mindset.

One practical way to integrate visualization and affirmation into daily life is to start each morning with a brief session. Spend five minutes visualizing a successful day while repeating affirmations aligned with your goals. This practice sets a positive tone for the day, preparing you mentally to tackle obstacles with determination and poise.

Consistent visualization exercises not only reinforce self-belief but actively enhance mental fortitude. Consider setting aside time each week to visualize overcoming specific challenges. As you repeatedly engage in these mental exercises, your brain adapts, focusing more on solutions rather than problems. This shift encourages a problem-solving outlook, fostering resilience.

Integrating these techniques into existing routines helps maintain a steady resilient mindset without feeling burdensome. Pair visualization with activities like brushing your teeth or commuting, turning routine actions into opportunities for mental strengthening. Similarly, affirmations can be woven into meditation practices, enhancing mindfulness and deepening their impact.

Beyond individual practice, visualization and affirmations hold value in professional settings. High-stress environments often test resilience, and these techniques offer simple yet effective tools for managing stress. Before meetings or demanding tasks, take a moment to envision positive outcomes and repeat affirmations that ground you in confidence. Such practices can transform apprehension into assurance, enabling professionals to navigate challenges with a composed demeanor.

While visualization and affirmations may initially present challenges, their benefits far outweigh the difficulties. Many find it initially hard to focus during visualization, wrestling with wandering thoughts. Starting with short sessions and gradually increasing duration can help build concentration. Similarly, vivid imagery may seem elusive initially but becomes more accessible with regular practice and creativity.

The rewards of consistent practice are substantial. Visualization and affirmations boost self-confidence, reinforcing the belief that one can tackle adversity effectively. These exercises enhance problem-solving skills by allowing exploration of different scenarios mentally, leading to more innovative solutions. Stress reduction is another significant benefit; visualizing calm, serene settings triggers relaxation responses in the body, easing tension and anxiety.

Moreover, visualizations aid in emotional healing by reframing negative experiences. Imagining positive outcomes and successful handling of past challenges promotes emotional resilience, reinforcing the notion that setbacks are stepping stones for growth.

Advanced practices can further refine these techniques, targeting specific mental processes and psychological challenges. Mental rehearsal, for instance, involves vividly imagining successful outcomes for future events. This practice stimulates neural pathways akin to physical practice, preparing the mind and body for real-life scenarios, such as public speaking or competitive sports.

Harnessing visualization to develop coping strategies proves particularly useful for individuals dealing with chronic stress or trauma recovery. Visualizing oneself managing stress effectively or navigating challenging emotions supports the creation of robust coping mechanisms.

Final Thoughts

Throughout this chapter, we've explored a variety of actionable exercises designed to build and strengthen resilience in both everyday life and professional environments. With a focus on daily practices such as morning mindset routines, reflection through journaling, and the use of affirmations and visualization techniques, these strategies aim to fortify mental clarity and emotional well-being. By integrating stretching, gratitude exercises, and self-assessment periods into our routines, we can enhance our emotional intelligence and adaptability. Moreover, visualization and affirmation provide powerful tools for transforming negative thought patterns and boosting self-confidence.

Implementing these resilience-building practices can lead to a transformative journey toward greater personal strength and mental fortitude. By consistently practicing these exercises, we cultivate a resilient mindset capable of navigating adversity with grace and determination. This foundation of resilience supports not only personal growth but also professional success, offering a balanced approach to managing stress and achieving goals. As we continue to engage with these techniques, they become ingrained habits that help us face life's challenges with optimism and poise, enhancing both our individual capabilities and our overall sense of well-being.

Chapter 16

Conclusion: The Journey Continues

T he journey of building resilience is a path of discovery and transformation. As we navigate the ups and downs of life, each experience contributes to our growth in unique ways. This transformative journey involves recognizing the strength within us and understanding how we can harness it to overcome challenges. Resilience isn't just about bouncing back from adversity; it's about embracing the process of learning and evolving with every step we take. In this chapter, we delve into the milestones that mark this journey, celebrating the triumphs and lessons that have shaped us along the way.

Here, we will explore the importance of reflecting on our achievements and how this practice strengthens our confidence. By looking back at what we've accomplished, we gain a deeper appreciation for our capabilities and build a foundation of self-belief. We'll discuss practical strategies, such as mindfulness and gratitude, which help individuals maintain focus and positivity even during tough times. Additionally, the chapter highlights the role of supportive relationships and feedback loops in fostering a culture of continuous improvement. Through these discussions, readers will discover pathways to reinforce their resilience, equipping themselves to face future adversities with courage and clarity.

Reflecting on Resilience Growth

In the journey of building resilience, recognizing milestones plays an essential role in highlighting the progress we make. These key moments serve as markers, indicating how far we have come and reinforcing our achievements on this challenging path. Recognizing these milestones allows us to see the moments when we have displayed strength and determination, which are often easy to overlook in the hustle and bustle of daily life. Each milestone, no matter how big or small, stands as a testament to our growth and commitment to overcoming adversity.

One way to recognize these milestones is by adopting practices that cultivate mindfulness. Mindfulness helps us stay present in the moment, allowing us to fully appreciate our progress without getting caught up in worries about the future or past struggles. Take a moment to reflect on what you have achieved so far: Did you navigate a difficult situation with calmness and clarity? Were you able to stand up for yourself when it mattered most? By identifying these instances of personal growth, we reinforce the idea that resilience is not just about enduring challenges but also about celebrating the strength we find within ourselves.

Reflecting on our achievements is another powerful tool in fostering a sense of accomplishment and strengthening confidence. When we take the time to look back at what we have successfully overcome, it serves as a reminder of our capabilities and enhances our belief in ourselves. Reflection is not just a passive activity; it's an active engagement with our experiences, where we learn from the obstacles we've faced and the strategies that worked best for us. It can be helpful to maintain a journal where you document your achievements and the feelings these victories evoke. This practice provides a tangible record of your growth, available to revisit whenever you need a boost of confidence.

Moreover, identifying small victories is crucial in recognizing personal strengths and encouraging ongoing resilience practices. In the grand scheme of things, these small triumphs may seem insignificant, but they are integral to the larger picture of personal development. Perhaps you managed to complete a task despite feeling overwhelmed, or maybe you maintained your composure during a tense discussion. Each of these instances is a victory worth acknowledging because they highlight the qualities that contribute to your resilience—persistence, courage, adaptability.

It's important to create a supportive environment that encourages the recognition of these small successes. Sharing your achievements with friends, family, or support groups can foster a sense of community and inspire others who may be on a similar journey. This communal celebration of milestones builds a network of encouragement and motivation, bolstering each member's commitment to their personal growth goals. For example, if someone has made progress in incorporating regular exercise into their routine, celebrating this achievement with peers could motivate them to continue developing healthy habits.

In acknowledging our progress and celebrating each milestone, we also pave the way for gratitude, which further enhances our resilience. Gratitude shifts our focus from what is lacking to what has been accomplished, nurturing hope and a positive outlook even during challenging times. By expressing gratitude for the growth we have experienced, we affirm our ability to adapt and thrive, regardless of circumstances.

Guidelines can be instrumental in helping individuals identify and celebrate milestones effectively. Begin by setting clear, achievable goals that align with your personal vision of growth. Use SMART (Specific, Measurable, Achievable, Relevant, and Time-bound) criteria to define what success looks like for you. Document these goals and review them regularly to track your progress. Recognize that every step forward, no matter how small, brings you closer to your overall objectives.

Additionally, it's essential to take proactive steps towards cultivating resilience. This might include developing assertiveness skills—standing up for yourself in challenging situations—or practicing self-compassion and forgiveness, both of which are vital for maintaining mental health and well-being. Engaging in activities that promote relaxation and stress relief, such as meditation or exercise, can also support this process by providing a much-needed outlet for emotions and tensions.

An effective strategy for maintaining momentum in your resilience-building efforts is to integrate reflection and celebration into your routine. Create rituals around these practices, such as monthly reflections or quarterly celebrations of accomplishments, to ensure they remain a regular part of your lifestyle. By embedding these activities into your life, you sustain the motivation needed to continue on your growth journey.

Continuous Development of Resilience Skills

At the heart of resilience lies the perpetual need for growth and adaptation. This journey is not a destination but an ongoing process that continually evolves as we encounter new challenges and opportunities. Viewing resilience this way requires a commitment to lifelong learning, which acts as a cornerstone in strengthening our capacity to cope with adversity and broaden our perspectives.

Commitment to lifelong learning enhances resilience by equipping individuals with diverse coping strategies. By continuously acquiring new skills and knowledge, we become better prepared to face unexpected situations, enabling us to adapt gracefully. For instance, engaging in online courses or workshops that focus on stress management techniques can provide practical tools to manage emotional upheavals. These educational experiences do not merely expand our intellectual horizons; they actively contribute to mental resilience by fostering flexibility in thinking and approach (McQuillen, 2024).

Moreover, lifelong learning encourages curiosity, keeping our minds agile and receptive to change. This expanded perspective helps us approach problems creatively, turning setbacks into stepping stones for further development. Through ongoing education, whether formally or informally, individuals cultivate the ability to view setbacks as learning opportunities instead of insurmountable obstacles. This mindset shift is pivotal, as it empowers people to navigate life's uncertainties with greater confidence and less fear.

A crucial part of developing resilience is effectively utilizing feedback loops. Engaging with constructive criticism and maintaining supportive relationships are vital in honing resilience skills. Feedback, when embraced positively, serves as a valuable tool for self-improvement and growth. Constructive criticism allows individuals to reflect on their actions and decisions, identify areas for improvement, and make necessary adjustments. This process not only improves personal and professional performance but also strengthens emotional resilience by reducing sensitivity to failure or criticism.

Supportive relationships play a significant role in reinforcing resilience, offering both encouragement and practical advice. Establishing a network of peers, mentors, or colleagues who provide honest and constructive feedback fosters a culture of continuous improvement. This collaborative environment nurtures resilience by emphasizing shared experiences and mutual support. For example, participating in peer review groups or mentorship programs offers opportunities for feedback exchange, bolstering individual confidence and skill development (*Resilience Redefined: Navigating Life with Personal, Social, and Feedback Strength*, 2023).

Guideline: When incorporating feedback loops, aim to maintain open communication channels that invite honest dialogue and foster trust. Regular check-ins and feedback sessions encourage growth and adaptability while building a resilient mindset.

Setting future goals is another critical component in the resilience-building journey. Goals serve as motivational anchors, providing direction and purpose even during challenging times. The process of setting and striving toward future objectives instills a sense of agency and determination that fuels perseverance. For instance, setting short-term and long-term goals related to career advancement or personal well-being can keep motivation levels high amidst difficulties. Achieving these goals reinforces self-efficacy, further enhancing one's capacity to tackle future adversities with renewed vigor.

Creating clear and realistic goals is essential, as they help individuals focus on what truly matters, minimizing distractions and confusion. A well-defined goal-setting strategy includes breaking down larger, long-term objectives into smaller, manageable milestones. This approach not only ensures steady progress but also provides opportunities to celebrate successes along the way, reinforcing resilience through acknowledgment of achievements.

Guideline: Develop a structured goal-setting framework that outlines specific, measurable, achievable, relevant, and time-bound (SMART) objectives. This clarity enables individuals to remain focused and motivated throughout their resilience journey, promoting consistent growth and adaptation.

Embracing change is integral to the continuous process of resilience. Change presents both challenges and opportunities, demanding adaptability and openness. Embracing change means accepting the inevitability of uncertainties and preparing to respond with agility. This proactive approach prevents stagnation and fosters innovation, driving individuals to rethink strategies and explore new possibilities. In doing so, people develop a stronger, more adaptable mindset capable of weathering the storms of life.

A positive attitude towards change encourages resilience by enabling individuals to anticipate and prepare for transitions. For instance, adopting a change-oriented mindset in the workplace might involve staying abreast of industry trends, seeking new roles or projects that challenge current abilities, and actively participating in stretching one's capabilities. This embrace of change builds confidence and fortifies resilience, equipping us to face life's twists with courage and ingenuity (McQuillen, 2024).

Guideline: Cultivate an atmosphere that welcomes change by nurturing a growth mindset and seeking out opportunities for expansion. Encourage reflection on past experiences to identify lessons learned, paving the way for more informed decision-making in future endeavors.

Gratitude for Growth and Embracing Change

Gratitude and adaptability are crucial components in enhancing resilience and fostering personal growth. Life is filled with challenges that can sometimes be overwhelming, but adopting a mindset of gratitude helps nurture hope and maintain a positive outlook, even during tough times.

Gratitude practices have been shown to enhance resilience by shifting focus from negative to positive aspects of life. By regularly expressing gratitude, individuals cultivate an appreciation for their life's blessings and develop a hopeful perspective. This positive outlook is vital in managing stress and adversity. For instance, when faced with a daunting work project or a challenging life event, taking a moment to reflect on the support received from colleagues or loved ones can help reinforce feelings of hope and encouragement. These practices allow individuals to remain optimistic, even when circumstances seem dire, helping them bounce back more effectively from setbacks. In essence, gratitude helps create a mental environment where resilience can thrive.

Furthermore, embracing change is an important practice in building confidence in personal resilience. Change is inevitable in life, and being adaptable means preparing oneself mentally and emotionally for these shifts. When individuals view change not as a threat but as an opportunity for growth, they begin to strengthen their resilient mindset. Consider, for example, a professional who has been laid off due to restructuring within their company. Rather than succumbing to despair, embracing this change could motivate them to explore new career paths or enhance their skills. This adaptive approach boosts confidence and prepares them for future changes, reinforcing their belief in their ability to handle life's unpredictability.

Understanding past experiences through reflection is another crucial element that contributes to better decision-making. By reflecting on previous experiences, both successes and failures, individuals gain valuable insights that inform their future choices. Reflection involves thinking deeply about past situations, understanding what worked well, what did not, and why. This process facilitates learning and growth, which are essential for developing resilience. It allows individuals to identify patterns, recognize strengths, and avoid repeating mistakes. For example, someone who successfully managed a personal crisis by seeking support from friends and family might recall this strategy during future challenges, knowing it contributed positively in the past. These reflections provide clarity and guide more informed decisions, leading to constructive personal and professional growth.

Moreover, incorporating reflection into daily routines can significantly enhance decision-making abilities. By setting aside time each day to contemplate recent events and decisions, individuals can better understand the outcomes of their actions and adjust accordingly. This practice leads to heightened self-awareness, enabling people to make choices that align with their values and goals. Through consistent reflection, individuals develop a deeper understanding of themselves, their motivations, and their capacities, all of which enhance their resilience.

While practicing gratitude, embracing change, and reflecting on past experiences independently contribute to resilience, their combined effect is transformative. Together, these practices foster a mindset equipped to handle life's adversities with grace and determination. Acknowledging the positives, adapting to changes, and learning from the past collectively build a fortified foundation of resilience, allowing individuals to navigate life's challenges confidently and grow personally.

Concluding Thoughts

Reflecting on the journey of building resilience, we have explored the importance of acknowledging small victories and cultivating a supportive environment. These elements serve as pivotal markers of progress, reminding us of our growth and reinforcing our determination.

Recognizing each milestone, whether it be maintaining composure during a tense moment or overcoming a challenging task, highlights the personal strengths we sometimes overlook. Through mindfulness and gratitude practices, we deepen our appreciation for these achievements, fostering a mindset that encourages further resilience. This reflection not only celebrates our past accomplishments but also prepares us to embrace future challenges with renewed confidence.

Looking forward, the ongoing development of resilience skills becomes essential in navigating life's uncertainties. Commitment to lifelong learning and openness to feedback broadens our adaptability, equipping us with diverse strategies to manage stress effectively. Additionally, setting clear goals and accepting change as an opportunity for growth fortifies our resilient foundation. By embracing these concepts, we cultivate a positive outlook and an agile mindset capable of transforming obstacles into opportunities. This optimistic approach empowers us to handle adversity with grace and determination, ultimately enhancing our mental strength and emotional well-being.

References

Chapter 1

ADD Resource Center. (2022, July 5). *Resilience: A process and a mindset.* Retrieved from https://www.addresourcecenter.com

Antonovsky, A. (1979). *Health, stress, and coping.* Jossey-Bass Publishers.

Britt, T. W., Shen, W., Sinclair, R. R., Grossman, M. R., & Klieger, D. M. (2016). How much do we really know about employee resilience? *Industrial and Organizational Psychology, 9* (2), 378-404. https://doi.org/10.1017/iop.2015.107

Davis, P. (2016, February 8). *5 myths about resilience.* Forbes. Retrieved from https://www.forbes.com/sites/pauladavislaack/2016/02/08/5-myths-about-resilience/

de Terte, I., & Stephens, C. (2014). Psychological resilience of workers in high-risk occupations. *Stress and Health, 30* (5), 353-355. https://doi.org/10.1002/smi.2627

Debunk Common Myths About Resilience - Steps to Leaps - Purdue University. (2018). Retrieved from https://purdue.edu/stepstoleaps/new/featured/well-being-tips/2024_0401.php

Fletcher, D., & Sarkar, M. (2013). Psychological resilience. *European Psychologist, 18* (1), 12-23. https://doi.org/10.1027/1016-9040/a000124

Johnson, J., Wood, A. M., Gooding, P., Taylor, P. J., & Tarrier, N. (2011). Resilience to suicidality: The buffering hypothesis. *Clinical Psychology Review, 31* (4), 563-591. https://doi.org/10.1016/j.cpr.2010.12.007

Maltby, J., & Hall, S. S. (2022). Less is more: Discovering the latent factors of trait resilience. *Journal of Research in Personality, 97* , 104193. https://doi.org/10.1016/j.jrp.2022.104193

Maltby, J., Day, L., & Hall, S. (2015). Refining trait resilience: Identifying engineering, ecological, and adaptive facets from extant measures of resilience. *PLOS ONE, 10* (7), e0131826. https://doi.org/10.1371/journal.pone.0131826

Maltby, J., Day, L., Hall, S., & Chivers, S. (2019). The measurement and role of ecological resilience systems theory across domain-specific outcomes: The domain-specific resilient systems scales. *Assessment, 26* (8), 1444-1461. https://doi.org/10.1177/1073191117738045

Price, R. B., & Duman, R. (2019). Neuroplasticity in cognitive and psychological mechanisms of depression: An integrative model. *Molecular Psychiatry.* https://doi.org/10.1038/s41380-019-0615-x

Wagnild, G. (n.d.). *Four myths about resilience.* Retrieved from https://www.resiliencecenter.com/things-to-read/healthy-and-resilient-aging/four-myths-about-resilience/

U.S Department of State. (2009, January 20). *What is Resilience?* Retrieved from https://2009-2017.state.gov/m/med/dsmp/c44950.htm

Yao, Z.-F., & Hsieh, S. (2019). Neurocognitive mechanism of human resilience: A conceptual framework and empirical review. *International Journal of Environmental Research and Public Health, 16* (24), 5123. https://doi.org/10.3390/ijerph16245123

Chapter 2

Bradley, J. (2023, July 4). *The Transformative Power of Positive Thinking: Shifting Your Mindset* . Medium. https://johncrestaniaffiliate.medium.com/the-transformative-power-of-positive-thinking-shifting-your-mindset-f2cacfaf121a

Dealing with Negative Thoughts and Cultivating a Growth Mindset | TrainSmart Australia . (2023, March 3). https://tsa.edu.au/dealing-with-negative-thoughts-and-cultivating-a-growth-mindset/

Dweck, C. S. (2006). *Mindset: The new psychology of success.* Random House.

Growth vs. Fixed Mindset: The Implications for Leadership and Innovation . (2023, October 3). Deliberate Directions. https://www.deliberatedirections.com/

growth-versus-fixed-mindset-implications-for-leadership-innovation/

Jeremiah. (2024, June 27). *It's All In The Mind: Growth Mindset Vs. Fixed Mindset* . Goalswon.com; GoalsWon. https://www.goalswon.com/blog/growth-mindset-vs-fixed-mindset

Sutton, J. (2019). *What is resilience and why is it important to bounce back?* PositivePsychology. https://positivepsychology.com/what-is-resilience/

Vacho, I. (2023, September 30). *Reframing Techniques: Resilience and Growth Through Altered Perspectives* . Medium. https://medium.com/@izo.vacho.creates/reframing-techniques-resilience-and-growth-through-altered-perspectives-fb9519d5666

Chapter 3

Cherry, K. (2023, December 31). *5 Key Components of Emotional Intelligence* . Verywell Mind. https://www.verywellmind.com/components-of-emotional-intelligence-2795438

Craig, H. (2019, January 30). *The Theories of Emotional Intelligence Explained* . PositivePsychology.com. https://positivepsychology.com/emotional-intelligence-theories/

Chowdhury, M. R. (2019, January 22). *What is emotional resilience? (+6 proven ways to build it)* .

PositivePsychology.com. https://positivepsychology.com/emotional-resilience/

Liu, Q., Jiang, M., Li, S., & Yang, Y. (2021, January 29). *Social support, resilience, and self-esteem protect against common mental health problems in early adolescence* . Medicine. https://www.ncbi.nlm.nih.gov/pmc/articles/PMC7850671/

Covapsychology. (2024, October 18). *Mastering Emotional Resilience: Effective Strategies for Tough Times* . Cova Psychology. https://covapsychology.com/blog/mastering-emotional-resilience-effective-strategies-for-tough-times/

Chapter 4

7 Steps to Manage Stress and Build Resilience | Office of Research on Women's Health . (n.d.). Orwh.od.nih.gov. http://orwh.od.nih.gov/in-the-spotlight/all-articles/7-steps-manage-stress-and-build-resilience

Davis, P. (2020, March 26). *How Adversity Makes You Stronger* . Forbes. https://www.forbes.com/sites/pauladavislaack/2020/03/26/adversity-makes-you-stronger/

Madeson, M. (2024, July 26). *Moving From Chronic Stress to Wellbeing & Resilience* . PositivePsychology.com. https://positivepsychology.com/chronic-stress/

https://bravanti.com/author/bpigroup. (2024, August 29). *The Relationship Between Change & Resilience* . Bravanti. https://bravanti.com/the-relationship-between-change-and-resilience/

Lifecoachtraining. (2023, July 12). *The Impact of Resilience and Mental Toughness on Personal and Professional Success* . Life Coach Certification Online. https://lifecoachtraining.co/the-impact-of-resilience-and-mental-toughness-on-personal-and-professional-success/

Chapter 5

American Psychological Association. (2020). Building your resilience. https://www.apa.org/topics/resilience

Bartholomew, K., Ntontis, E., & Drury, J. (2022). Resilience in the face of adversity: Individual, group, and societal pathways to adaptive functioning. Current Opinion in Psychology, 45, 101308. https://doi.org/10.1016/j.copsyc.2021.12.006

Calm Blog Team. (2023, September 5). Mental strength: 8 ways to build resilience. *Calm Blog.* https://www.calm.com/blog/mental-strength

Explore Psychology. (2017, October 8). 3 great positive thinking techniques. *Explore Psychology.* https://www.explorepsychology.com/positive-thinking-techniques/

Gliapko, L. (2024, August 21). Practical strategies on how to increase mental toughness. *Indiana Center for Recovery*. https://www.treatmentindiana.com/practical-strategies-on-how-to-increase-mental-toughness/

Mental Health Center of San Diego. (2024, October 21). How to build emotional resilience | Tips for mental strength. *Mental Health Center of San Diego*. https://mhcsandiego.com/blog/how-to-build-emotional-resilience/

MsEd, K. C. (2024, October 6). 3 Great Positive Thinking Techniques. Explore Psychology. https://www.explorepsychology.com/positive-thinking-techniques/

National Institutes of Health. (2022, August 8). Emotional wellness toolkit. *National Institutes of Health (NIH)*. https://www.nih.gov/health-information/emotional-wellness-toolkit

NYC Integrative Psych. (n.d.). The transformative power of positive thinking. *NYC Integrative Psych*. https://www.integrative-psych.org/resources/the-transformative-power-of-positive-thinking

Oshri, A., Topple, T. A., & Carlson, M. W. (2019). Resilience and the brain: A neurobiological perspective on positive adaptation to adversity. Behavioral Sciences, 9(4), 34. https://doi.org/10.3390/bs9040034

Chapter 6

7 Steps to Manage Stress and Build Resilience | Office of Research on Women's Health . (n.d.). Orwh.od.nih.gov. http://orwh.od.nih.gov/in-the-spotlight/all-articles/7-steps-manage-stress-and-build-resilience

Ackerman, C. (2017, October 28). *Coping: Dealing with Life's Inevitable Disappointments in a Healthy Way* . Positive Psychology. https://positivepsychology.com/coping/

Algorani, E. B., & Gupta, V. (2023, April 24). *Coping mechanisms* . PubMed; StatPearls Publishing. https://www.ncbi.nlm.nih.gov/books/NBK559031/

Chowdhury, M. R. (2019, January 22). *What is emotional resilience? (+6 proven ways to build it)* . PositivePsychology.com. https://positivepsychology.com/emotional-resilience/

Group, W. T. (2024, October 21). *How to Build Mental Resilience: Proven Strategies for a Stronger Mind | WTG* . Williamsburgtherapygroup.com; Williamsburg Therapy Group. https://williamsburgtherapygroup.com/blog/how-to-build-mental-resilience

Newman, K. (2016, November 9). *Five science-backed strategies to build resilience* . Greater Good. https://greatergood.berkeley.edu/article/item/five_science_backed_strategies_to_build_resilience

Chapter 7

Arlinghaus, K. R., & Johnston, C. A. (2018, December 29). *The Importance of Creating Habits and Routine* . American Journal of Lifestyle Medicine. https://doi.org/10.1177/1559827618818044

Mayo Clinic Staff. (2020, October 27). *How to Build Resiliency* . Mayo Clinic. https://www.mayoclinic.org/tests-procedures/resilience-training/in-depth/resilience/art-20046311

Newman, K. (2016, November 9). *Five science-backed strategies to build resilience* . Greater Good. https://greatergood.berkeley.edu/article/item/five_science_backed_strategies_to_build_resilience

Positive Mindset: Strategies for Developing a Growth-Oriented Attitude . (n.d.). Www.graygroupintl.com. https://www.graygroupintl.com/blog/positive-mindset

Positive Thinking: Optimism, Gratitude and Happiness . (2010). Pursuit-of-Happiness.org. https://www.pursuit-of-happiness.org/science-of-happiness/positive-thinking/

Robins, E. (n.d.). *The secret benefit of routines. It won't surprise you. - Headspace* . Www.headspace.com. https://www.headspace.com/articles/the-secret-benefit-of-routines-it-wont-surprise-you

Chapter 8

7 Steps to Manage Stress and Build Resilience | Office of Research on Women's Health . (n.d.). Orwh.od.nih.gov. http://orwh.od.nih.gov/in-the-spotlight/all-articles/7-steps-manage-stress-and-build-resilience

Bautista, E. (2024, November 27). *Building Resilience: Thriving in the Face of Workplace Challenges* . Griffinhill.com; Griffin Hill. https://blog.griffinhill.com/building-resilience-thriving-in-the-face-of-workplace-challenges

Center, B. A. C. (2023, August 9). *How Conflict Can Help Strengthen Your Relationship: 5 Strategies to Enhance Connection* . Bay Area CBT Center. https://bayareacbtcenter.com/how-conflict-can-help-strengthen-your-relationship-5-strategies-to-enhance-connection/

Gupta, D. (2023, January 27). *Resilience Training in the Workplace (+Examples, Tips) | Whatfix* . The Whatfix Blog | Drive Digital Adoption. https://whatfix.com/blog/resilience-training/

McQuillen, B. (2024, August 21). *Building Resilience and Adaptability in Times of Change and Uncertainty* . Ignitehcm.com; Ignite HCM LLC. https://www.ignitehcm.com/blog/building-resilience-and-adaptability-in-times-of-change-and-uncertainty

Otting, K. (2024, June 6). *Interaction Management Associates* . Interaction Management Associates. https://

imamediation.com/blog/the-surprising-benefits-of-conflict-personal-growth-and-stronger-connections

Chapter 9

Dagenais, C. (2024, January 2). *The Art Of The Comeback: Building Resilience In The Face Of Setbacks* . Forbes. https://www.forbes.com/councils/forbescoachescouncil/2024/01/02/the-art-of-the-comeback-building-resilience-in-the-face-of-setbacks/

Emanuele, G. (2020, March 23). *Galen Emanuele | Team Culture & Leadership Keynotes* . Galen Emanuele | Team Culture & Leadership Keynotes . https://galenemanuele.com/blog/how-to-deal-with-failures-setbacks

Embracing Failure: How Our Greatest Lessons Come from Setbacks - Well Nourished Integrative Psychiatry - Lakewood, CO . (2024, May 20). Well Nourished Integrative Psychiatry. https://wellnourishedpsych.com/blog/embracing-failure-how-our-greatest-lessons-come-from-setbacks/

Houston, E. (2019, April 9). *What is Goal Setting and How to Do it Well* . PositivePsychology.com. https://positivepsychology.com/goal-setting/

Mending Minds. (2024). *Reframing Failure: Harnessing Setbacks for Mental Resilience* . Medium; Medium. https://medium.com/@MendingMinds/

reframing-failure-harnessing-setbacks-for-mental-resilience-0d8c03f40bb4

Turning failures into opportunities for growth and success with resilience . (2022, February 8). Joeymycoach.com. https://www.joeymycoach.com/en/publications/turning-failures-into-opportunities-for-growth-and-success-with-resilience/

Chapter 10

Cooks-Campbell, A. (2022, July 15). *Triggers: Learn to Recognize and Deal With Them* . BetterUp. https://www.betterup.com/blog/triggers

Godreau, J. (2024, February 16). *Emotional Triggers: Why They Matter & How to Manage Them Effectively* . Mindful Health Solutions. https://mindfulhealthsolutions.com/emotional-triggers-why-they-matter-how-to-manage-them-effectively/

How to be more empathetic: 8 exercises to develop empathy — Calm Blog . (n.d.). Calm Blog. https://www.calm.com/blog/how-to-be-more-empathetic

Sutton, J. (2020, September 16). *Developing Empathy: 8 Strategies & Worksheets to Become More Empathic* . PositivePsychology.com. https://positivepsychology.com/empathy-worksheets/

Scott, E. (2022, December 23). *5 Emotion-Focused Coping Techniques for Stress Relief* . Verywell Mind.

https://www.verywellmind.com/emotion-focused-coping-for-stress-relief-3145107

University of Rochester Medical Center. (2019). *Journaling for Mental Health* . Rochester.edu; University of Rochester Medical Center. https://www.urmc.rochester.edu/encyclopedia/content.aspx?ContentID=4552&ContentTypeID=1

Chapter 11

Ackerman, C. (2017, January 18). 22 *Mindfulness exercises, Techniques & Activities for Adults* . Positive Psychology. https://positivepsychology.com/mindfulness-exercises-techniques-activities/

How to Manage Stress with Mindfulness and Meditation . (2021). Mindful. https://www.mindful.org/how-to-manage-stress-with-mindfulness-and-meditation/

Keng, S. L., Smoski, M. J., & Robins, C. J. (2011). *Effects of Mindfulness on Psychological health: a Review of Empirical Studies* . Clinical Psychology Review. https://doi.org/10.1016/j.cpr.2011.04.006

Mayo Clinic Staff. (2022, October 11). *Mindfulness exercises* . Mayo Clinic. https://www.mayoclinic.org/healthy-lifestyle/consumer-health/in-depth/mindfulness-exercises/art-20046356

Treatment, M. (2023, December 1). *The Benefits of Using Mindfulness-Based Practices for Emotional*

Regulation . Mississippi Drug and Alcohol Treatment Center. https://mississippidatc.com/the-benefits-of-using-mindfulness-based-practices-for-emotional-regulation/

Zandi, H., Amirinejhad, A., Azizifar, A., Aibod, S., Veisani, Y., & Mohamadian, F. (2021, May 31). *The effectiveness of mindfulness training on coping with stress, exam anxiety, and happiness to promote health* . Journal of Education and Health Promotion. https://doi.org/10.4103/jehp.jehp_616_20

Chapter 12

Magic, G. (2020, June 28). *Building Resilience: Strategies for a Stronger Mindset in Life and Work* . Go Magic. https://gomagic.org/building-resilience-strategies-for-a-stronger-mindset-in-life-and-work/

Bakic, H., & Ajdukovic, D. (2021, January 1). *Resilience after natural disasters: the process of harnessing resources in communities differentially exposed to a flood* . European Journal of Psychotraumatology. https://doi.org/10.1080/20008198.2021.1891733

Malala's Nelson Mandela Lecture: A Call to Global Action for Education – Nelson Mandela Foundation . (n.d.). Www.nelsonmandela.org. https://

www.nelsonmandela.org/news/entry/malalas-nelson-mandela-lecture-a-call-to-global-action-for-education

Malala Yousafzai: 21st Nelson Mandela Annual Lecture | Malala Fund . (n.d.). Malala.org. https://malala.org/newsroom/malala-yousafzai-21st-nelson-mandela-annual-lecture

Ma, C., Qirui, C., & Lv, Y. (2023, December 14). *"One community at a time": promoting community resilience in the face of natural hazards and public health challenges* . BMC Public Health; BioMed Central. https://doi.org/10.1186/s12889-023-17458-x

Rood, A. (2023, June 15). *The Path to Emotional Wisdom: Building Resilience* . Medium. https://deliberateself.medium.com/the-path-to-emotional-wisdom-building-resilience-7f0f28a26cef

Chapter 13

Can Social Media and Online Communities Be Good for Us? | Psychology Today . (n.d.). Www.psychologytoday.com. https://www.psychologytoday.com/intl/blog/the-science-of-fandom/202303/can-social-media-and-online-communities-be-good-for-us

Learn. (2023, June 26). *Why is the support of a friend or family member important in mental health care? - Learn to Live* . Learn to Live. http://

www.learntolive.com/insights/why-is-the-support-of-a-friend-or-family-member-important-in-mental-health-care

Oksanen, A., Celuch, M., Reetta Oksa, & Savolainen, I. (2024, August 2). *Online communities come with real-world consequences for individuals and societies* . Communications Psychology. https://doi.org/10.1038/s44271-024-00112-6

Suttie, J. (2017, November 13). *Four Ways Social Support Makes You More Resilient* . Greater Good. https://greatergood.berkeley.edu/article/item/four_ways_social_support_makes_you_more_resilient

Southwick, S. M., Sippel, L., Krystal, J., Charney, D., Mayes, L., & Pietrzak, R. (2016, February 1). *Why are some individuals more resilient than others: the role of social support* . World Psychiatry. https://doi.org/10.1002/wps.20282

Social Connection Builds Resilience . (2020, November 16). Anne Grady Group. https://www.annegradygroup.com/social-connection-builds-resilience/

Chapter 14

CDP, S. (2024, January 29). *Building Resilient Teams: Strategies for Thriving in Uncertain Times* .

Cochran, Cochran & Yale. https://ccy.com/building-resilient-teams-strategies-for-thriving-in-uncertain-times/

Farrell, J. (2024). *How to Build and Lead Resilient Teams* . Maven.com; Maven Learning, Inc. https://maven.com/the-growth-lab/building-resilience

Good, in. (2024, January 30). *SuccessCOACHING | Customer Success Training for CSMs* . SuccessCOACHING | Customer Success Training for CSMs. https://successcoaching.co/blog/building-team-resilience-in-good-times-and-tough-times

Leis, M., & Wormington, S. (2024, July 3). *The 12 characteristics of a good leader* . Center for Creative Leadership. https://www.ccl.org/articles/leading-effectively-articles/characteristics-good-leader/

Maven. (n.d.). *Maven: 10 Effective Strategies Building Your Team's Resilience* . Maven.com. https://maven.com/articles/build-team-resilience

https://bravanti.com/author/bpigroup. (2024, October 15). *Resilient Leadership: 18 Core Attributes of Unstoppable Leaders* . Bravanti. https://bravanti.com/resilient-leadership-core-attributes-of-unstoppable-leaders/

Chapter 15

100 Journal Prompts For Self-Growth With Examples - Brahmas Natural Incense . (2023, December

4). D4c.site. https://brahmas.co/blog/100-journal-prompts-for-self-growth-with-examples/

Develop Fortitude: Positive Affirmations for Mental Health . (2024, May 23). Ability plus Mental Health Clinic. https://abilityplusmentalhealthllc.com/positive-affirmations-for-mental-health/

Koschalk, K. (2023, October 24). *Journaling for Personal Growth: The Impact of Journaling for Self-Improvement* . Rosebud.app; Rosebud. https://www.rosebud.app/blog/journaling-for-personal-growth

Ryan Zofay Author Coach & Speaker . (2024, August 28). Ryan Zofay. https://ryanzofay.com/morning-routine-checklist/

Sutton, J. (2018, May 14). *5 Benefits of Journaling for Mental Health* . Positive Psychology. https://positivepsychology.com/benefits-of-journaling/

With, R. (2024, November 30). *Our Mental Health* . Our Mental Health. https://www.ourmental.health/resilience/boost-mental-resilience-with-visualization-practical-strategies-for-toughness

Chapter 16

Bradley, J. (2023, June 13). *Gratitude and Personal Resilience: Bouncing Back Stronger with a Thankful Attitude.* Medium; Lampshade of ILLUMINATION. https://medium.com/lampshade-of-illumination/

gratitude-and-personal-resilience-bouncing-back-stronger-with-a-thankful-attitude-c588bb9e0c59

Bradley, J. (2023, June 17). *Gratitude and Personal Reflection: Navigating Life's Crossroads with Thankfulness*. Medium. https://medium.com/@johnbradley1/gratitude-and-personal-reflection-navigating-lifes-crossroads-with-thankfulness-de710402b33c

Embrace the Journey: The Significance of Personal Growth Milestones . (n.d.). Personal Growth. https://personalgrowth.com/personal-growth-milestones/

McQuillen, B. (2024, October 18). *Building a Resilient Workforce: Strategies for Continuous Learning and Adaptation in a Changing World* . Ignitehcm.com; Ignite HCM LLC. https://www.ignitehcm.com/blog/building-a-resilient-workforce-strategies-for-continuous-learning-and-adaptation-in-a-changing-world

Resilience Redefined: Navigating Life With Personal, Social, and Feedback Strength . (2023). Psichi.org. https://www.psichi.org/page/282Eye-Resilience-Redefined

The Importance of Celebrating Milestones in Recovery . (n.d.). Www.townsendla.com. https://www.townsendla.com/blog/celebrating-milestones-in-recovery